Concepts of
INTELLIGENCE

Concepts of
INTELLIGENCE

THOMAS J HALLY

iUniverse, Inc.
Bloomington

Concepts of Intelligence

iUniverse books may be ordered through booksellers or by contacting:

iUniverse
1663 Liberty Drive
Bloomington, IN 47403
www.iuniverse.com
1-800-Authors (1-800-288-4677)

ISBN: 978-1-4759-4145-6 (sc)
ISBN: 978-1-4759-4146-3 (ebk)

Library of Congress Control Number: 2012913911

Printed in the United States of America

iUniverse rev. date: 10/03/2012

Dedicated to my dear wife,
Guadalupe García Hally

"Two things fill my mind with ever-increasing wonder
and awe: the starry heavens above me
and the moral law within me."

~ *Immanuel Kant*

CONTENTS

ACKNOWLEDGMENTS

I would first and foremost like to thank the Editor of the *Mensa International Journal*, Kate Nacard. Kate was that special person everyone hopes will enter their lives. She took a long shot chance and "hired" me as her feature-article writer for the *MIJ* in May of 2007. Without Kate's enthusiasm, empathy and encouragement, things would be very different for me today than they are. Thanks are also in order for Doctor Patrick M. O'Shea, Professor of Music at St. Mary's University of Minnesota and the President of the International Society for Philosophical Enquiry. He is a former Editor of the Society's journal, *Telicom.* Patrick also took a chance, choosing me as Editor-in-Chief of *Telicom* in November 2007. I stayed on as Editor until April 2010. I learned how to write well editing *Telicom.* Lastly, but certainly not least, a "thank you" to my precious wife, Guadalupe, for her love, her patience, and for the fantastic job she does as my artist and proofreader.

INTRODUCTION

Six years ago I would have told anyone he was "crazy" if he had told me I would be the Feature Articles Writer for the *Mensa International Journal.* Now, after more than five years of experience writing for the *MIJ*, I can only say "Wow." Why Wow?—because I had the opportunity of a lifetime in my hands and it became a tangible reality. I have literally been able to "reach out and touch" the better part of more than 110,000 Mensans throughout the world. Some of these Mensa members have taken the trouble to write to me asking for a pdf copy of this or that article for their Web site while others critique me. Still others just write to say "Hello" or to tell me that his or her favorite article is "such and such." It's always a great feeling knowing that someone out there actually *has* a "favorite" and I am not being, well—ignored!

Mensans always state their mind. Another positive quality they have is to listen to, and not shut up and "turn off" a co-participant in an intellectual—and sometimes "heated"—discussion or a friendly conversation. This "open-mindedness with a backup reserve," as I like to call it, is the primary reason why I am always grateful when a Mensan takes the time to share his or her ideas with me. Those who have written have always been encouraging, and none have been rude. There is no telling what I might write after corresponding with a fellow Mensan.

This current tome is a collection of my favorite articles in the general area of "concepts of intelligence": psychology, psychometrics, computers and related areas. Human intelligence is discussed as well as artificial intelligence. I have also included an article on animal intelligence. The hours researching and "putting together" each of these articles was both time-consuming and exciting and, hence, not in the least bit boring. I hope you enjoy reading *Concepts of Intelligence* as much as I did writing it. Concepts of Intelligence is intended for everyone. It is not only a book that pretends to challenge you and get you thinking, it is also your ideal reference book to the mind. And it will answer some of those "mysterious" questions that may have piqued your curiosity as you are growing with or have grown up with and matured with the forever-young "Computer Age." There are no IQ tests or other gimmicks within the pages of Concepts of Intelligence. If you are looking for a test *similar* to a Mensa IQ test, visit the Mensa International Web site at www.mensa.org and take the "Mensa Workout."

Although it took me five years to write "Concepts of Intelligence," I can almost guarantee it will take a lot less time to read.

Enjoy!

May 18, 2011

July 19, 2012 (Second Edition)

Thomas J Hally

1

POLYGLOTTISM

Ask anyone you know to define the word *polyglot* and most will say "a person who speaks many languages." A polyglot is defined by most dictionaries as a person who has a speaking, reading, or writing knowledge of several languages. The etymology of the word comes from the Greek *poluglottos*, meaning many tongued. Dictionaries all agree that a polyglot handles several languages — but what defines several?

Someone who speaks two languages including his native tongue is considered bilingual. There is a debate, however, whether one who speaks three languages should be called a polyglot or a trilingual. According to most researchers on the subject, a true polyglot emerges when that person can fluently speak three languages as well as his native tongue. Does one define a person as a polyglot when they have the ability to utter "Have a nice day" in seven foreign languages? Obviously not . . . In order for someone to be considered a speaker of a certain language, one needs a moderately solid base vocabulary as well as an average grasp of spelling, pronunciation, and grammar of the language spoken.

It is not unusual for someone to speak two or three languages, but, beyond that, language fluency becomes a relative rarity. Being a polyglot puts someone in the company of people like Pope John Paul II, famous for his language skills. When we speak of persons who can handle a dozen languages or more, we use the term "hyper-polyglot," which was coined in 2003 by linguist Richard Hudson. The most famous hyper-polyglot was probably Guiseppe Mezzofanti, a 19th century Italian Cardinal, who was reputed to speak seventy-two languages (although other histories have him speaking thirty-eight languages fluently, fifty dialects fluently, while also having proficiency in many other languages with a lesser fluency). It is said that Mezzofanti could remember a word infallibly after having heard it only once. If one assumes that each language has, say, 20,000 words, he would have to learn an incredibly unrealistic word-per-minute for twelve hours daily during a five and one half year period. How likely is that? Yet, he was tested constantly by critics, and all were impressed. One of them even called him "The Devil" because of his uncanny skill.

Polish-born German linguist Emil Krebs was reputedly conversant in over 100 languages. His brain was removed in 1930 by researcher Oscar Vogt, and to this day it is kept in the C. and O. Vogt Institute for Brain Research of the Heinrich Heine University, Düsseldorf, Germany. His private library of over 3500 volumes and writings is in approximately 120 languages and is kept in the National Library in Washington, D.C. Other famous hyper-polyglots include Ziad Youssef Fazah (1954—Present), a Liberian, who has at least some notions of almost 60 languages. He was considered the world's greatest polyglot *(Greatest Living Linguist)* by the 1993 UK edition of the Guinness Book of World Records. Paul Robeson (1898-1976), an American actor, athlete, singer, writer, and political and civil rights activist, could speak more than 20 languages, including Yiddish, Russian, German, Welsh, Spanish, and several African languages.

Did Mezzofanti, Krebs, and Robeson have extraordinary brains or are hyper-polyglots ordinary people who manage to do something extraordinary through motivation and hard work?

After one has learned a second language, the third, fourth, and so on languages come easier, especially if the languages are related. The more one knows about how languages work the more expert at learning them one becomes. Reference is made to Jeanette Littlemore and her expansion of Howard Gardner's "Theory of Multiple Intelligences." According to researcher Littlemore, there is yet another intelligence that she calls *metaphoric intelligence*. The use of metaphor pervades

3

all language and communication to such a degree that it is one of the chief ingredients in language learning. Stating examples like "mouth" of the river, "eye" of the needle and "heart" of the matter as commonplace expressions which represent metaphorical extensions of parts of the body. "Frozen" and "novel" metaphors are those which aid a person in language learning, and, indeed, in all academic learning. Frozen metaphors are those that are in common use in the language and novel metaphors are the ones in which ideas are combined in new ways. Effective use of frozen and novel metaphors is what goes into the making of a polyglot. What is a frozen metaphor to a native speaker is a novel metaphor to a language learner when he or she stumbles upon it for the first time. Littlemore hints that divergent thinking as well as "loose analytical reasoning" may play a major role in language learning.

Some researchers conclude that there is such a thing as a talent for learning languages, while others are of the opinion that polyglots just work hard to learn three or more languages and talent has nothing to do with it. Those people with high verbal skills do better on language based tests, but are, in reality, no smarter than the rest of us.

Ask yourself, "How many languages can I learn?" In theory, there is only a time factor involved for the capacity to learn human languages. Experts in linguistics say that most of us have the potential to become hyper-polyglots.

2

BIRTH ORDER AND INTELLIGENCE

Interest in the relationship between birth order and extraordinary achievement dates back to at least 1874 and Francis Galton's book, *English Men of Science: Their Nature and Nurture.*[1] As the pioneer of eugenics, Galton chronicled the lives of 180 eminent scientists from various fields and was able to collect birth order data from ninety-nine of these subjects, revealing that forty-eight percent of them were first-born sons or only sons.[2]

Countless studies have confirmed Galton's conclusion, and interest in birth order and eminence continues unabated. The correlation between primogeniture status and eminence is likely limited to certain types of scientific achievement, since later-born children are more inclined to become revolutionary leaders and scientists, and they may be, in fact, far more creative than first-borns.

In 1973, Lillian Belmont and Francis Marolla published family size, birth order and intelligence test (Dutch version of the Raven Progressive Matrices) data from nearly the entire population of nineteen-year-old Dutch men (386,114 subjects). The study revealed that the children from larger families tend to do poorer on intelligence tests and educational measures than their counterparts from smaller families, even when social class is controlled. First-borns consistently scored better on the Raven than did later-born children, and with few exceptions, there was a gradient of declining scores with rising birth order, so that first-borns scored better than second-borns, who, in turn, scored better than third-borns, etc. An increase in family size usually indicated a decrease in RPM performance within any particular birth order position. For example, a third born child from a three-child family would have been expected to score higher than a third born child from a four-child family, and a third born child from a five-child family would have been expected to score even lower.

There have been different approaches with different conclusions since the Belmont-Marolla study, and *"Longitudinal studies,"*[3] which track individual families over time, reveal that there is no relationship between birth order and IQ. However, the tendency for large families to produce lower IQ children stands firm regardless of the research project. The *Admixture hypothesis* purportedly accounts for the causal link between birth order and IQ. Proponents of this hypothesis argue that other factors, such as parental IQ or socio-economic status may be responsible for both larger families and low IQ, making it appear in *Cross-sectional studies[4]* as though birth order causes lower IQ. Instead, it is possible that families with lower IQ members tend to have more children. If true, the mean IQ for any given population would gradually decline. To the contrary, mean IQ scores are actually rising with each successive generation.[5,6]

According to Galton's study, birth order may effect eminence because primogenitures would be more likely to have the financial resources to continue their education, first borns had the advantage of being treated as companions by their parents, implying more undertaking of responsibility than their younger siblings, and first born sons would get more attention and better nourishment in families with limited financial resources.

The Resource Dilution Model[7] offers a simple explanation both for higher IQ scores of first-born children and for their overrepresentation among the college population of the eminent. It depends upon three assumptions: 1) Parental resources are finite, 2) Additional siblings reduce the share of parental resources received by any one child; 3) Parental resources have an important effect on their children's educational success.

The Confluence Model[8] was proposed by R.B. Zajonc and Markus (1975) and Zajonc (1976; 2001), and explains the first-born IQ advantage in terms of the ever-changing intellectual environment within the family. It uses a simple formula to compute the relative advantages and disadvantages of various factors such as later-born sibling competition for parental attention, explaining the Belmont-Marolla finding that first borns from smaller families have higher IQs than first borns from larger families. First borns are also exposed to more adult-level vocabulary than their siblings, effecting their performance on verbal scales of intelligence tests. The linguistic immaturity of first-born children's brothers and sisters also gels with the finding that children from larger families have lower IQ scores.[9]

First borns (and older siblings in general) often have to answer questions and explain things to their younger siblings. It is believed this act of tutoring helps the older children to cognitively process information. With rare exceptions, younger siblings do not get the opportunity to tutor their brothers and sisters, effectively explaining why only children usually do not have a higher IQs than first borns.

If first-borns do indeed have higher IQs than their siblings, this fact may not be important. Recent studies suggest that intelligence is not the most important factor in the achievement of eminence. Several studies have indicated that personality traits such as consciousness and openness to experience are up to ten times more important than IQ. Additionally, in studies showing a statistically significant advantage for first borns, birth order accounts for only one percent of the variance in IQ. First born IQ advantage is tiny—about one point higher than the second sibling, two points higher than the third, and so on. A minute difference of one or two points on an IQ test is meaningless, since it is within the margin of error, and is highly unlikely to be a significant predictive factor in the pursuit of greatness in any intellectual endeavor.[10]

3

CREATIVE GENIUS OR PSYCHOTIC?

A genius is one who has made a significant contribution to mankind through the use of his or her intelligence and creativity. The definition of a madman, however, is somewhat blurry. The idea of a positive correlation between genius and insanity has long fascinated people, given that the boundaries between abnormal and supernormal are arbitrary and somewhat ill-defined. Eccentric behavior may be seen by some as just an anomaly and perceived as madness by others.

Two traits of psychotic individuals, latent inhibition and fantasy proneness, go hand in hand with creativity. Latent inhibition, a certain degree of intelligence, and fantasy proneness all factor into a theory of how creativity and psychoses are intertwined. Poetry is,

10

undeniably, one of the highest forms of creative art, and some of the most creative poets are the ones who exhibit the most signs of psychoses. Fantasy proneness can be equated with having an "overactive imagination." Auditory and visual hallucinations are symptoms of fantasy prone people and not only schizophrenics and manic depressives. It is sometimes a very difficult task differentiating a psychotic from a highly creative person due to the strong connection between the traits.

Proponents of the genius/madness link will point to a number of research studies done on eminent historical figures such as Vincent Van Gough, Winston Churchill, and Edgar Allan Poe, who all suffered from bi-polar disorder. John Forbes Nash, mathematician and Nobel Laureate in Economics and writer Jack Kerouac were paranoid schizophrenics. Less prominent individuals with psychiatric conditions have been studied to see if they are more creative than the "normal" population. In a study conducted by Hagop Akiskal, of the University of Tennessee in the United States, 750 individuals with depression, bipolar disorder, and schizophrenia were tested, and it was found that ten percent of the mildly to moderately affected were creative writers or artists. A study in Denmark by Ruth Richards and Dennis Kinney revealed that creativity was significantly higher in the bipolar subjects than in the control group. But Dr. Kenneth Lyen, a pediatrician at Mount Elizabeth Hospital in Singapore says "Thus there is a small body of evidence to support a link between creativity and bipolar disorders, but this is not the same as saying between genius and madness."[11] And later he states

"To sum up, here is a modified quote 'You don't have to be mad to be a genius . . . but it helps'"[12]

This brings up an interesting question: Should all mental illness be treated with medication? Many artists and scientists suffering from psychiatric disorders refuse medication because they claim it blunts their creativity; although some bipolar patients absolutely require medicine due to the ever-present danger of suicide.

Certain types of mental disability may have compensatory affects. The dyslexic, for example, compensates for his difficulty with language by increasing his or her process of visual perception and creativity. Cubist Pablo Picasso suffered from dyslexia, so does Hollywood comedian and talk show host Jay Leno. Mild manic patients can display accelerated thinking, verbal fluency, and be very apt at punning; yet those individuals with severe mania lose all these positive affects, "deleting" all productive thinking and creativity. Some researchers concur that the link between genius and a small percentage of schizophrenics boils down to a particular gene called DARPP-32—dopamine and cyclic AMP-regulated phosphoprotein—which works as a neurotransmitter and links genius to madness. Three quarters of any given population inherit a version of the DARPP-32 gene, which enhances the brain's activity to think by improving the information processing of the prefrontal cortex, orchestrating thoughts and actions. Dr. Daniel Weinberger, from the U.S. Institute for Mental Health, believes the gene translates into a hindrance during a severe schizophrenic episode.

At the beginning of the 20th century, psychologist William James and some of his contemporaries emphasized the positive aspects of certain psychological disorders, and speculated that a sufficient degree of intellect could combine with special talent into extraordinary creativity. Mild mania and hallucinations can combine for new creative thought processes, and even be shown to elevate IQ scores. Paranoia, in a mild form as well as depression that is not severe can serve as "checks" to excesses in thought and action, and are also powerful for creativity. Stanford University researchers Connie Strong and Terrence Ketter, M.D., using personality and temperament tests, found that healthy artists are more similar to persons with depression than in the general population.

During the early stages of mental disorders such as schizophrenia there are often feelings of deep insight, and a sense of mystical knowledge and religious experience. Chemical changes occur in the brain that make the individual more open to incoming stimuli from the surrounding environment. The ancient Greeks believed that creative inspiration ("afflatus") was achieved through altered states of mind such as "divine madness." The creative "daemon"—particularly poetry and art—has often been considered as being part and parcel of the "dark depths of irrationality" while maintaining a tenuous connection to reality.

4

ARE WE SMARTER THAN OUR ANCESTORS?—THE FLYNN EFFECT

Professor of political science and moral philosophy, James Flynn of the University of Otago in Dunedin, New Zealand, is one of the world's leading psychology theorists. In 1984, he received a package from an academic in The Netherlands which contained results of the IQ test Ravens Progressive Matrices. P.A. Vroon, the academic who sent Flynn the package, did not know how to score the tests, but Flynn did. He noticed a huge jump in the scores of Dutch males over the previous generation, and decided to check on data from around the world. The answer always came up the same: IQs were rising dramatically. In 1994, the "Flynn Effect" was the name coined by authors Herrnstein and Murray as an explanation for the increasing IQ scores in more than 30 industrialized and developing nations.

The 73 year-old professor *emeritus* found that IQ had improved in the 20th century at the rate of an incredible three points per decade. Earlier researchers had failed to notice this trend because IQ scores are always calculated with respect to the average score of the present group. For example, if the average IQ is 100 and a person scores 20 percent above average his IQ would be 120; but if that person's score were compared with the IQ of a person a generation earlier, his IQ would be about 130. Flynn was the first psychometric researcher to make this cross-generational comparison. He discovered that the largest gains appear on IQ tests that measure fluid intelligence (*Gf*) rather than crystallized intelligence (*Gc*). The eponymous Flynn Effect shows that the average IQ in America on tests like the Ravens Progressive Matrices seems to have risen fifteen points between 1930 and 1980; and, in all countries for which data has existed, IQ scores have been increasing.

But to what extent do IQ tests measure raw intelligence versus learning versus some other factor correlated with intelligence? Scholars around the world are still researching this question, but Professor Flynn believes that the hypothesis that best fits the results of his study is that IQ tests do not measure intelligence but rather correlate with a weak causal link to intelligence. Flynn is certain that the increase in IQ is actually an increase in abstract problem solving rather than intelligence. We must re-think exactly what we mean by intelligence.

Because populations experience IQ gains over time, we must constantly re-standardize IQ tests so that subjects are not scored against inaccurate IQ norms. The use of obsolete norms can cause problems, particularly when comparing scores between different groups and different populations. A widely held hypothesis is that people lose fluid intelligence over time. In his book, *What is Intelligence? Beyond the Flynn Effect* [13] he discusses a mystery that has baffled IQ researchers for decades—"Are we really smarter than our ancestors?"

Older people were raised in an era when the general level of intelligence was lower. Professor Flynn showed that if a person's IQ is calibrated for the period in which they grew up, an old person scores just as well as a young one. The reason that the graying population doesn't do as well on IQ tests as young people is not because older people are stupid, rather the younger generation simply has had a head start.

Flynn believes that detaching logic from the concrete defines the mark of intelligence in the modern world. We have created the tools and the environment to maximize these scores. Seventy-five years ago there were no televisions, no computers, no cell phones and, in most cases, no automobiles. Programming a VCR or texting a message on a cell phone requires a minimum of abstract savvy. The time-tested, practical ideation and solutions of our parents and grandparents has given way to technology and science.

Professor Flynn's "multiplier effect" is integral to this hypothesis. Simply stated, the more adults (especially higher IQ adults) there are to children, the more likely the young ones will be positively influenced. According to Flynn, the hypothesis that the offspring of two intelligent people are likely to have more "good genes" for intelligence does not convincingly account for the astronomical rise in IQs.

Over time, one would expect that that the opposite ends of the Bell Curve would stretch as humans with the highest—and lowest—IQ scores mate and reproduce. Furthermore, individuals with lower IQs are having more children than their higher IQ counterparts. Would this not *lower* the average IQ?

Flynn has opened a Pandora's Box of paradoxes. He believes that seventy-five percent of the score on an IQ test is due to nurture and twenty-five percent of the score is due to nature. Yet, studies show a strong correlation between the IQs of identical twins raised apart which is higher than those of fraternal twins raised in the same household. The Flynn Effect illustrates the difficulty of comparing test results over time, but says little about the validity of tests within a given generation.

Professor Flynn believes that some of us have reached the upper level of our cognitive functions. Various factors include single parenthood and low birth rates; and we have, simply, become "lazy." Scandinavia, in especial, has been affected more by this "dumbing" trend, or "leveling off," and not those nations studied in the developing world.

The consequences of mental lethargy might be that we, as Mensans, could be called upon to re-think the modern world as we help ourselves function at a higher intellectual level. Isn't one of the original goals of Mensa to foster human intelligence"?

5

HOWARD GARDNER'S THEORY OF MULTIPLE INTELLIGENCES

In 1983, American psychologist Howard Gardner proposed a theory that had as its goal to broaden the traditional definition of intelligence. He felt that the concept of intelligence, as it had been defined by IQ tests, was too narrow, not capturing the ways in which humans can excel. Howard Gardner's theory was, briefly, that we do not have one *general intelligence* that governs our thinking, but instead we have *multiple intelligences,* each part of an independent system in the brain. His emphasis was on the range of human abilities that exist across cultures.

When Howard Gardner's book *Frames of Mind: The Theory of Multiple Intelligences* appeared, it apparently answered many questions for many people, creating individual *cognitive profiles.* First he identified and introduced us to seven different types of intelligences, starting with *linguistic intelligence* which he calls sensitivity to the meaning and order of words. People who are good at reading, writing, memorizing words and dates and people with a facility for foreign languages fit into this category. Those with *logical-mathematical intelligence* are good at abstractions, inductive and deductive reasoning and are numerically adept. Formal logic is controlled by mathematical intelligence while the other forms of this intelligence are under the command of verbal intelligence. *Musical intelligence,* simply stated, is the ability to understand and create music. Rhythm, music, and hearing are the keys to this type of intelligence. Those endowed with musical intelligence often use songs or melodies to learn or memorize information; and may do their best work with the radio or a CD playing. One who has the gift of *spatial intelligence* has the ability to think pictorially and to perceive the world accurately, altering it or recreating it in their mind or on canvas. It is no wonder that artistic geniuses such as Picasso or Dalí fit neatly into this framework. Many of those with high mathematical-logical intelligence are weak spatially and many with high spatiotemporal ability are weak in math skills. (This may well come as a surprise to some.) *Bodily-kinesthetic intelligence* is the ability to use one's body to solve problems. It is the ability to coordinate one's bodily movements in physical activity. Those who exhibit this intelligence to a greater extent include mimes, dancers, athletes (especially basketball players) and actors. The sixth and seventh intelligences on Gardner's list are similar in that they both involve introspection and comprehension of others. Most of us have the ability to perceive and understand other individuals to a lesser or greater degree. *Interpersonal intelligence* allows us to work effectively with our colleagues and neighbors. Educators, salespeople, religious and political leaders, and social workers all need well developed interpersonal intelligence if they are to be adept at what they do. The last of Howard Gardner's original multiple intelligences is *intrapersonal intelligence.* It allows us to understand ourselves and to appreciate our own feelings, fears, and motivations. This working model helps us to use information about ourselves to regulate our lives.

In *Frames of Mind,* Gardner treats the personal intelligences almost as one unit because of their close association in most cultures; but he argues that it still makes more sense to think of two forms of personal intelligence. He believes that the seven intelligences rarely operate independently, tending to complement the other skills, augment them, and to solve problems.

Since his original multiple intelligences listing in 1983, there has been discussion as to the inclusion of other "candidates" to the original seven. *Naturalist intelligence*, or the ability to recognize, categorize and draw upon certain features of the environment, was worthy, in Gardner's eyes, to be included with the other seven. Gardner excluded a possible *spiritual intelligence* because of its inability, as he perceived it, to codify criteria in comparison with the other intelligences. *Existential intelligence* is the capacity to reflect on life, death and ultimate meaning. It was left out due to lack of identifiable areas in the brain that would specialize for this. Finally, *moral intelligence* was eliminated because it is normative rather than descriptive.

Criticism of the theory of multiple intelligences centers on the criteria Gardner employs. *Do all intelligences involve symbolic systems?* How and why are particular criteria to be applied? Howard Gardner admits there is an element of subjective judgment involved. *Does his conceptualization of intelligence hold together?* There are researchers, scholars, and, of course, psychometricians who view intelligence as, in effect, what is measured by IQ tests. They argue for a correlation of different abilities and "*g*" or a general intelligence factor. Gardner believes it is not yet possible to know how far intelligences actually correlate. Recent developments such as Robert Sternberg's advancement of the *triarchic model* share Gardner's dislike of the standard intelligence theory. The triarchic model, the componential (analytic), experiential (creative) and contextual (practical) facets of intelligence, differs from Gardner's theory in as much as it does not stress the particular material that a person possesses. Musical intelligence and bodily-kinesthetic intelligence are more appropriately seen as "talents" since they are not normally needed to adapt to life's demands. *Is there sufficient evidence to support the conceptualization of multiple intelligences as Howard Gardner proposes it?* He is criticized strongly because the theory derives from his own intuition and reasoning and not from full empirical research. There is no effective set of tests[14,15] to identify and measure the different intelligences. Yet Gardner eschews tests because he believes they lead to labeling and stigmatizing.

While there are serious questions surrounding Howard Gardner's theory of multiple intelligences, it has proven to be useful in education. The researchers at Project SUMIT (Schools Using Multiple Intelligences Theory), under the lead of Mindy Kornhaber, have examined a number of these schools and have concluded that there have been significant gains in respect to SAT scores. To the extent that Howard Gardner's theory has helped educators, it has been judged to be useful.

6

MOCTEZUMA'S REVENGE—CHOCOLATE CAN BOOST YOUR IQ!

The people of Mexico have been cultivating chocolate for thousands of years; and they have been responsible for its globalization. *Xocoatl* in the Aztec language, or Nahuatl, means "bitter water," *xoco* meaning "bitter" and *atl* for "water." Hernán Cortez, the Spanish Conquistador who defeated the Aztec nation between the years 1519 and 1521, brought samples of *Xocoatl,* in the form of cocoa beans, with him to the courts of Europe. The Europeans sweetened and refined the process of making chocolate. It has been said that Montezuma (or Moctezuma, as he is known

24

as in Spanish and Nahuatl) would drink many goblets of bitter chocolate before visits to his harem. Thus chocolate, since its "discovery," has been known to be an aphrodisiac. The cocoa bean was used by the Aztecs as monetary exchange, and the more chocolate one had the richer he was. By the 1700s, the delightful beverage and food had reached the United States. Thus chocolatl became universalized. Today, chocolate is probably the most popular dessert and snack in the Western World.

Chocolate can affect the "pleasantness" circuits in the brain and therefore not only tastes good in the mouth, but certain brain circuits can be influenced by tasty choices. Several studies suggest that consuming foods rich in flavonols, a naturally occurring nutrient abundant in fresh cocoa, may improve the brain's multiple roles. Scientists believe that these benefits may have important implications for learning and memory, such as healthy brain functioning throughout several life stages. This is particularly beneficial for older adults, who suffer so much from dementia, and for others who may be in situations where they may be cognitively impaired, such as sleep deprivation or fatigue. Commercially available cocoa is low in flavonols. Mars Inc, maker of Mars Bars is producing flavonol-rich versions of chocolate bars and cocoa. Other companies are following suit.

Doctor Henrietta van Pragg, of the Salk Institute for Biological Studies, carried out a study of the effect of epichatechin, a flavonol, on mice. She reported that the compound influenced the hippocampus, a gland in the brain that affects the memory. When epichatechin was added to their food, she said the mice demonstrated improved skills in solving and remembering a maze compared to mice who did not consume the compound.

There has been much research done on chocolate and its health benefits in general. It is known that chocolate releases phytosteral, a plant substance that mimics human sex hormones; and we have learned that dark chocolate has antioxidants and cardiovascular benefits. Now there is another reason why we should give into our chocolate cravings—chocolate makes you smarter! Dr. Bryan Raudenbush, of the Wheeling Jesuit University in West Virginia, found that eating milk chocolate (my favorite) may boost brain power. To assess the effects of various types of chocolate on volunteers, Dr. Raudenbush's study required them to consume, on four separate occasions, 85 grams of milk chocolate, 85 grams of dark chocolate, 85 grams of carob, a chocolate-like bean, and nothing (the control condition). After fifteen-minute digestive periods, the volunteers completed a variety of neuropsychological and computer-based tests which had been designed to evaluate cognitive performance. This included memory, attention span, problem-solving, and reaction time. Dr. Raudenbush and his colleagues found that the composite scores for verbal and visual memory were much higher for milk chocolate than for the others. In his study, Dr, Raudenbush measured volunteers via the Profile of Mood States (POMS) and the NASA Task Load Index. The researchers believe that the digestion of chocolate helps cognitive performance by the release of glucose and an ensuing increased blood flow to the brain. Included in chocolate that gives your brain that extra lift are theobromine, phenethylamine, and caffeine. All help in the brain's concentration and focus.

A study by Professor Ian Macdonald of the University of Nottingham, England found that consumption of a cocoa drink rich in flavonols, a key ingredient of dark chocolate, boosts blood flow to the brain for two to three hours. Increased flow to these areas helps better one's performance in certain tasks and raises general attention. Professor Macdonald said "Acute consumption of the particular flavonol-rich cocoa beverage was associated with increased grey matter flow for two to three hours.[16]"

According to Jeannine Virtue, a freelance journalist who writes on a variety of topics relating to ADHD, memory, depression and stress, dark chocolate is the best. Dark chocolate contains several natural stimulants (including caffeine) which enhance focus and concentration, have powerful antioxidant properties and stimulate the production of endorphins to help improve mood. She notes that one half ounce of dark chocolate daily has more benefit than milk chocolate or white chocolate (which has no beneficial properties and is not really chocolate, but cocoa butter, milk and sugar) The processed chocolates, according to Virtue, do not really elevate brain power.[17]

The only down side, it seems, from eating chocolate is that chocolate packs in the calories—loads of them—so eating chocolate in moderation is advised. Whether yours is a milk chocolate drink or bar or a piece of dark chocolate, enjoy a small amount daily. For me there is nothing better with breakfast than a small *Carlos V,* a delicious milk chocolate bar prepared and consumed in the land where *Xocoatl* was first born. It helps me get me day off to a good start and feeling in the right place at the right time.

7

MEN WITH SMARTS ARE MEN WHO WIN HEARTS

All of us recognize "sexy" when we see it—sure! It's really not hard to detect, right?

For a more objective idea, let's take a look at what the Oxford English Dictionary has to say: sexy, adj. 1. Containing or characterized by explicit sexual content; erotic, risqué; bawdy, saucy; 2. a. Of a person (esp. a woman): sexually attractive or alluring; (also) sexually charged, highly sexed; b. Of a personal attribute, thing, etc.: characterized by sexuality or sexual appeal; sexually attractive, stimulating, or suggestive; c. colloq. In extended use: appealing, stimulating; liable to excite interest.[18]

So, let's talk about sex . . . shall we?

Geoffrey Miller is a widely-respected Assistant Professor of Psychology and an evolutionary psychologist in the tradition of Richard Dawkins, Daniel Dennett, and Steven Parker. Professor Miller has worked at the University of New Mexico, Albuquerque, since 2001.[19] He is known for his research which focuses on evolutionary psychology and sexual selection, and states that our minds evolved as courtship machines, and not only as survival machines. He believes that the human mind's mechanisms evolved as an attempt to attract and entertain potential sexual partners; thereby switching from a survival-centered to a courtship-centered vision of evolution. Miller attempts to show how we can further understand the mysteries of the mind and, in support of his views on evolution and sexual selection, he wrote *The Mating Mind: How Sexual Choice Shaped the Evolution of Human Nature*.

Reviving Darwin's theory that sexual selection has been critical in human evolution, Miller emphasizes the self-expressive aspects of human behavior such as art, morality, language, and creativity. Adaptive design features suggest that these traits evolved through mutual mate choice to advertise not only intelligence, creativity, and moral character, but also heritable fitness. His theory makes testable predictions and sheds additional light on the human condition: our cognition, motivation, communication, sexuality, and culture: in short, our mores.

One of Professor Miller's conclusions posits that men with the highest IQs are generally considered as more attractive and also have the healthiest sperm. He headed a research project that centered on a study of 400 Vietnam War veterans who were put through extensive mental tests and were also asked to provide samples of their sperm. Those men who scored highest on the battery of intelligence tests boasted high counts of healthy sperm, while those who scored lower on the IQ tests had lower sperm counts and unhealthy samples. The overall conclusion drawn by Miller was that sperm quality was in direct correlation with intelligence or "brain quality." He believes that the two traits have evolved together as a way to advertise healthy genes.

Language, intelligence, self confidence, humor, kindness, and selflessness have evolved because they are attractive to the opposite sex. Physical attractiveness or beauty plays an all important role initially in attracting a mate, but can quickly leave that "dolt of a male peacock" with his feathers ruffled if beauty is all he has to offer a woman. The object of his attempted wooing may feel disappointed when she realizes that the handsome individual before her is a complete "dud." On the other hand, *any* woman who is looking for a "quickie" or a "one night stand" may well choose a physically attractive man over an average-looking "Joe," regardless of positive or negative character traits. Women who choose life mates based *solely* on male beauty are generally considered *shallow* or lacking in good judgment.

The self-expressive aspects of art, morality, language, and creativity have proven to be elusive in their survival value, but their adaptive design features do indeed suggest they evolved through mutual mate selection.

Humor, though not directly linked to intelligence is, however, considered by many women as an indicator of a sharp mind and, coincidentally, many women consider humor as an indicator of male honesty. Speaking from a common sense point of view, a woman is not likely to be impressed by a sour puss of a man. A good sense of humor (GOSH) appears to be a prerequisite for a male partner.

Women rate funny guys as more intelligent than their dour counterparts, according to a finding presented on April 1, 2009 at the British Psychological Society's Annual Conference in Brighton. In the study, Kristofor McCarty of Nortumbria University asked forty-five heterosexual women to rate a series of men's autobiographical descriptions. The men who described themselves humorously were rated as significantly more intelligent than those whose descriptions were devoid of humor.

"Kristofor McCarty said 'A quick browse of the lonely hearts ads will confirm that women look for a good sense of humour in a potential partner—our research may explain why this the case . . .

'The findings provide evidence that women use humour as an indication of a guy's intelligence. Intelligence is a very attractive quality as a clever man should be more able to provide for his offspring. But guys be warned: not just any gag will do. We discovered that the humour must be genuinely funny for the man to be judged as more intelligent.'"[20]

While women appear to prefer a man who can make them laugh, psychologists suggest that the same does not hold true when the tables are turned. Men are generally not attracted to humorous women.

Ladies, put on your silliest thinking caps and seriously consider the outrageous possibilities. Are you willing to spend a good part of your life with an intelligent clown, or would you prefer that nitwit "hunk" who lives next door.

8

PHRENOLOGY: PROTOSCIENCE/
PSEUDOSCIENCE

In the final years of The Enlightenment, Austrian physician Franz Joseph Gall (1758-1828) pioneered the idea that different mental functions are located in different parts of the brain (1796).[21] Thus, phrenology was born, from φρήν, *phrenos*, "mind;" and λόγος, *logos* meaning "word," "reason." Gall's eloquently-titled work, *The Anatomy and Physiology of the Nervous System in General, and of the Brain in Particular,* propagated the principles of phrenology. The brain was the organ accountable for the propensities and faculties, with each part being responsible for a particular mental faculty. Gall's and his colleague's, Johann Spurzheim (1776-1832), theory was proselytized throughout

Europe and the United States. Briefly stated, moral and intellectual faculties are innate, the brain is composed of as many particular organs as there are propensities in human nature; and, most importantly, the form of the head or cranium represents the form of the brain, thus reflecting the relative development of its differing organs. Gall's controversial theory centered on the shape and size of the head and its protuberances. He initially formulated that there were twenty-seven organs on the surface of the brain which affect the contour of the surface of the skull. Shared by members of the human species were the instinct of reproduction, the carnivorous instinct and the tendency to murder; guile, vanity, "amativity" (or the love and friendship instinct), circumspection, memory, the organ of religion as well as the organ of perseverance and obstinacy, etc. Spurzheim, who coined the term *phrenology*, expanded the organs to thirty-seven in number, to include the virtues popular at the time. This cornucopia of instincts or tendencies was detailed on the famous "heads of china" produced by Fowler and Wells Company of New York, circa 1848.

Early in the 19th century, phrenology grew at a rapid pace. When phrenology was at its peak of popularity, in the 1820s – 1850s, palpitations of the skull with fingertips and palms were used by practitioners to determine the aptitude of a young man for a particular profession and the likelihood of a criminal to reciivate. These measurements and evaluations were used by politicians and protopsychometricians, respectively, to determine one's aptness for office (usually self determined beforehand) and the intelligence of a given individual. Gall gained support in scientific and political communities. He was seen as a secular savior in an environment dominated by many and variegated philosophies in a world where the main enemies to rationalization were religion, subjectivity and autocracy. The present day proponents of phrenology believe that the phrenological "snake oil salesmen," or charlatans of the time, abused "The Science," as the modern followers call it, with phrenological parlors, which were more appropriately suited for such avocations as astrology and chiromancy; and that, unfortunately, this practice gave phrenology a bad name, staining it as a real science.

Phrenology gave birth to other pseudoscientific schools such as craniology, the classification according to race, criminal temperament and intelligence; anthropometry, the documentation of facial characteristics of criminals; typology, a 20th century character classification according to body type; and psychognomy, a pseudoscience developed by Paul Bouts (1900-1999), a Belgian Catholic priest and scientist. Bouts ideas were based on typology and graphology, and his work continues today through the Dutch PPP Foundation (*Per Pulchritudinem in Pulchritudene*). In 1983, London psychologist Peter Cooper founded the London Phrenology Company to revive interest in phrenology.

Such devices such as a caliper for measuring the skull, tapes, and the Phrenology Machine were used by the late 19th century and early 20th century. The machine worked in the following way: the patient would sit in a chair and a helmet with sensing rod connections and switches would be lowered onto his head, measuring the bulges in the skull and finally printing out 160 statements on a rubber belt. These early printouts were used to determine a patient's personality and intelligence. The Phrenology Machine is preserved in the Museum of Questionable Medical Devices, in Minneapolis, Minnesota in the United States.

The modern day phrenologists believe that "The Science" gives a new dimension to the ancient adage, "Know Thyself."

9

ARE BEAUTIFUL PEOPLE MORE INTELLIGENT?

Dr. Satoshi Kanazawa, an evolutionary psychologist of the London School of Economics, blogged that numerous experiments over the years have shown that people tend to rate attractive people as more intelligent and more competent than unattractive people.[22]

Many sociologists and social psychologists are convinced of the old adages "Beauty is only skin deep" and "Beauty is in the eyes of the beholder." They dismiss the widespread perception that beauty correlates highly with intelligence as "bias," "stereotyping," or the "halo effect"[23] and lacking factual basis. Yet modern evolutionary psychology has shown that neither of these aphorisms is entirely true. The conclusion that beautiful people are more intelligent is drawn from four assumptions:

1. Men who are more intelligent are likely to attain higher status than men who are less intelligent;
2. Higher status men are more likely to mate with more beautiful women than lower status men;
3. Intelligence is heritable;
4. Beauty is heritable.

If these four assumptions are empirically true, then it logically follows that beautiful people are, indeed, more intelligent than their less attractive peers.[24] The conclusion makes the correlation between beauty and intelligence a theorem. A general female preference for intelligent males with higher income potential paired with a general male preference for attractive females become covariants over time.[25]

The theorem also claims that, in cross-cultural studies, there is a general consensus in the judgment of beauty. Indeed, this may be a fact, since the degree of Western media exposure seems to have no influence on people's perception of beauty. As an example, look at the racial and ethnic diversity of the winners of the annual Miss Universe and Miss World competitions. Standards of beauty appear to be innate rather than arbitrary, culturally specific and idiosyncratic. Thus, the theorem contends that standards of beauty are an integral part of human nature—even babies seem to smile more readily when physically attractive people smile at them. The authors of the KK theorem, Satoshi Kanazawa and Jody L. Kovar, inform us that there is a computer program which has the ability to digitally average human faces, assigning a single score for physical attractiveness, and correlating these scores with scores assigned by human judges. Beauty, therefore, appears to be an *objective* and *quantitative* attribute of individuals like height and weight.[26]

Furthermore, there is a correlation, according to Kanazawa and Kovar, between beauty and intelligence through assortive mating; more intelligent men are likely to be more attractive than less intelligent men, and more attractive women are likely to be more intelligent than less attractive women. If beauty and intelligence is inherited from both parents, the extrinsic correlation between beauty and intelligence in children will be even stronger than if intelligence is heritable only through the father and beauty is inherited through only the mother. Kanazawa and Kovar explain that the theory is purely deductive and not a comprehensive description of complex reality; it therefore leaves out much of what the authors posit as fact. They inform us that their theorem is purely scientific and logical, yet it is not a prescription of how to treat or judge others. Moreover, such a derived behavioral prescription would be an example of the "naturalistic fallacy."[27]

If the assumptions are logically a theorem, PhDs, other highly-educated people and most Ashkenazi Jews should be absolutely gorgeous. This assumption, however, is uniform and rigid, since these groups run the gamut of physical attractiveness as the rest of humanity.

Dr. Kevin Denny[28] believes that the KK theorem, given certain regularities about assortive mating and the heritability of intelligence and that of beauty, is a logical fallacy and the theorem that beautiful people are more intelligent is debatable. Denny contends that since "high status" changes over time, that which was attractive or intelligent to a Neanderthal, for example, certainly differs from attractiveness and the measure of intelligence in the twenty-first century. The same holds true for those Goya and Rubens models who posed nude. They might be considered as "too fat" or "unattractive" in today's modeling industry. Denny states, "The correlation of genes associated with beauty and intelligence may be complicated if the indicated genes are pleitropic, that is, they affect multiple phenotypic traits."[29] Beauty is subject to change over time, and the beautification industry attests to the fact that more intelligent people are more likely to have cosmetic surgery because they are wealthy.

If it *is* a fact that attractive people have greater self-confidence than unattractive people, this may account for their sometimes-higher wages. An individual's perceived beauty or height may be correlated with self esteem. Therefore, an attractive appearance and self-confidence may have *independent* effects on earnings and *assumed* high intelligence. In cases such as these, the strongest support appears to indicate discrimination on the part of the employer on the basis of taste. The relationship between attractiveness and intelligence is generally positive, but highly non-linear, with positive association declining at medium levels of intelligence and flattening out.

Judit Polgár, a 33-year old beauty of Jewish-Hungarian descent, achieved the title of Chess Grandmaster at the age of 15 in 1991. She was, at the time, the youngest person to earn that status. Polgár is considered as the world's eighth best chess player and the greatest female chess player in history. Judit Polgár has an IQ of 170. Dorota Rabczewska aka Doda Elektoda was ranked, in 2007, as Poland's second most beautiful woman. Formally a singer with the band "Virgin," she has since become a solo act. When she joined Mensa in 2004, her IQ was measured at 156.

Albert Einstein immediately comes to mind as contradictory to the KK theorem or the exception that proves the rule. With his long, grey, bushy hair, coupled with a good-natured clown-like appearance, he had the confidence and intellect to become one of the greatest geniuses in the history of science. Was his relative physical unattractiveness the reason why he was "assigned" a *relatively* conservative IQ of 160 . . . ? It is a hackneyed story and almost a cliché, but, considering the principles of eugenics, Irish playwright and 1925 Nobel Prize winner in literature, George Bernard Shaw was supposedly asked the following question by his lover, dancer Isadora Duncan: "With my body and your brains what a wonder it [our child] would be." "Yes, replied Shaw, but what if it had my body and your brains?"

The measuring of intelligence and other variables such as beauty and height is a fundamental research endeavor amongst social psychologists and evolutionary psychologists alike, stirring the interest of scholars and causing much controversy. The Kanazawa-Kovar claim that beautiful people are more intelligent is theoretically suspect because the evidence does not support it.

10

DOES GRAY MATTER MATTER MORE
THAN WHITE MATTER MATTERS?

The brains of men and women differ in size, architecture, and function. Men and women exhibit different behavioral patterns because their brains are constructed from very different genetic blueprints. The brain is made primarily of two different types of nerve tissue: *gray matter* and *white matter*. Gray matter is a brownish-grey tissue composed of cell bodies, dendrites (processes from nerve cells that conduct impulses towards the cell body) and supportive tissue. White matter is white-colored tissue consisting chiefly of myelinated nerve fibers. Myelin speeds the conduction of nerve impulses and is found around the axons (sites for the generation of nerve impulses) of certain nerve fibers and formed in the peripheral nervous system.

A 2005 University of California at Irvine study found that there are significant differences in the areas where men and women manifest their intelligence. The study revealed that women have ten times more white matter related to intellectual skills than men, while men have six and one-half times more gray matter related to intellectual skills than women.

Gray matter, in both the male and female brains, represents cerebral information processing centers, while white matter serves as the networking and connections of these processing centers.

Parts of the frontal lobe, where the decision and problem-solving functions take place, are proportionately larger in women as is the region that governs the emotions. Other studies have noted that the female hippocampus, a major area involved in memory function, also is proportionately larger in women than in men. Eighty-four percent of gray matter regions and eighty-six percent of white matter regions involved in intellectual performance in women are found in the brain's frontal lobes. Compare this to forty-five percent and zero percent for men, respectively. The gray matter that accounts for male intellectual performance is distributed throughout more of the brain; hence, men and women process information in very different ways: Men think more with their gray matter, and women think more with white matter. General human intelligence appears to be based on the volume of gray matter in certain regions that are located throughout the brain, thus making it highly unlikely that there exists a *single* "intelligence center," such as the frontal lobe.

The UC Irvine study found that eighty-four percent of gray matter regions and eighty-six percent of white matter regions involved in intellectual performance in women were found in the brain's frontal lobes. Men have proportionately larger parietal cortices than women. The parietal cortex is the area of the brain that processes signals from the sensory organs and is involved in space perception. The amygdala region, which controls emotions and social and sexual behavior, is also larger in men.

Men tend to outperform women in spatial awareness tasks such as navigation and mental rotation of objects and on tests of mathematical reasoning. Women score higher than men at remembering landmarks on maps, discrediting women's reputations as poor map readers. Females also excel in "emotional intelligence." Young girls generally have more language fluency than do boys; use more extensive vocabularies; exhibit better reading skills; and express themselves better linguistically than their male counterparts, using more complex sentences. Traditional feminine gender roles include such attributes as being nurturing, affectionate, warm and caring. Differing sharply, masculine characteristics generally show tendencies of aggressiveness, power and assertiveness. Nicholas Wade of *The New York Times* wrote:

In general, there is greater male variance in IQ. That is, although average IQs are identical in men and women, there are fewer average men than women and more men than women at both extremes of the bell curve.

While twice as many men as women populate the extreme right side of the intelligence scale (or "Bell Curve"), where the genius-level IQs run, the extreme left of the scale—where one finds the lowest IQs—is also where twice as many males as females are found. No single neuroanotomical structure determines general human intelligence (the *g*-factor), and different types of brains may perform equally well on IQ tests.

While males have more confidence than females in their overall cerebral prowess—including those of below average intelligence—women oftentimes underestimate their brain power, even some very bright women! Conceit and overbearing pride are unattractive human qualities, but self-confidence is a very useful and admirable trait.

As we know, IQ tests challenge a variety of skills yielding scores that are used as a measure of intelligence However, IQ tests are *not* good indicators of one's *native* intelligence, since they can vary from one test to the next. IQ test scores may increase or decline as we grow older.

11

ARE NIGHT OWLS MORE CREATIVE?

Did Benjamin Franklin have it wrong when he said "Early to bed and early to rise makes a man healthy, wealthy, and wise"?

When are you most productive—the morning time, in the afternoon or at night? If you are not a morning person, take heart. Recent studies suggest that "night owls" are more likely to be creative with bright ideas and a good deal of lateral thinking. Scientists can't fully explain why evening people seem to be more creative, but suggest it could be flexibility or adaptation to living different from the conventional 9 a.m. to 5 p.m. types. Nocturnal types diverge in life's experience with their inclination for living outside the norm. This may encourage the development of a non-conventional spirit and the ability to find alternative and original solutions.

Mariana Giampietro and G. M. Cavallera of the Department of Psychology of the Catholic University of the Sacred Heart in Milan studied 120 men and women of varying ages in creative thinking exercises. "Night-owl" types aced a series of tests, while morning and afternoon-type people had to struggle to get scores over 50 percent. The test evaluated degrees of morning and evening disposition. The test subjects were first required to draw a picture. In the second activity, "incomplete shapes," the subjects added lines to create pictures out of straight and curved lines, and they were asked to title the pictures. Finally, the group members were presented with 30 pairs of vertical lines and told to create pictures and title them. Giamprieto and Cavallera discovered that age does not curtail creativity.

Hans Van Dongen, associate research professor at the Sleep and Performance Center of Washington State University, was one of the scientists who discovered the biological explanation between morning and evening types. He and his colleagues found that a small group of brain cells called suprachiasmatic nuclei emit signals to the body synchronizing the time of day. This biological clock is two hours ahead in morning types and two hours behind in evening types. This internal clock may be partly explained by genetics, which was an unexpected finding regarding creativity on biological grounds—especially for night owls.

Van Dongen has suggested that evening people might be more extroverted than morning people. Voltaire, one of humanity's greatest minds, was renowned for sleeping in. Other night owls include novelists James Joyce and Marcel Proust—and ex-British Prime Minister Winston Churchill was also night owl.

Research has shown that a large percentage of US adults go to bed after midnight. And, many Asian adults and a good number of Europeans are also "burning the midnight oil." Many night owls have challenged society's moral judgments with science to back them up, and severe night owl problems such as "Delayed Sleep Phase Disorder" are genetic symptoms, not just peculiarities. The disorder is characterized by extreme difficulty falling asleep before the dictates of one's biological clock actually require it. Extreme cases cannot sleep before 6:00 a.m. and have a tendency to wake up at 10:00 a.m., or even later.

Depending on one's personality and environment, a morning work schedule may not be ideal for those of us who experience a late-night mental surge of energy. It is important to find what works for you; those of us who aren't suited to early rising usually can be more productive by utilizing the quiet evening hours. Yet, if poorly managed, sleeping late can lead grogginess and lost, wasted days. Sleeping too much is an unhealthy habit, and it is more harmful the older one gets. The maximization of creative productivity is influenced by the natural peaks of personal energy cycles, and age is no exception to this rule. Researchers at the Environmental Epidemiological Unit at Southampton

General Hospital found that, in a study of 129 men and women over age 65, night owls had the largest incomes, the greatest access to cars, and, of all things, the most indoor toilets.

Teens tend to be night owls. On weekends, when the pressure of work or school is not a factor, working adults wake up on an average of an hour later, while teens can sleep hours more, waking up at around 10:00 a.m., and sometimes much later.

So what does this mean for the average not so average Joe or Jane citizen like you and me? Should we try to alter our biological clock to fit a noon to 4:00 a.m. schedule, or should we simply be productive using our "nighttime creativity" in the morning, afternoon or at whatever time that is most convenient and practical for us? Shouldn't we just set our biological alarm clock to our own comfort level and relax and let our brain do the job of being creative? We can't help but succeed.

Good "night"!

12

DUMBO IS NOT SO DUMB, NOR IS KOKO NOR WAS ALEX

In 1911, American psychologist Edward Lee Thorndike updated studies he had started in 1898 and brought them together in a single volume, *Animal Intelligence: Experimental Studies.* He started from the hypothesis that rational thought and ideation in humans was merely an extension of animal intelligence. Concepts, feelings of relationship, association by similarity, and even reason itself followed from a simple increase in number, delicacy and complexity of associations. Thorndike went on to examine the learning curve of monkeys for evidence of ability to learn by imitation or inference. He concluded that there was scant support for the hypothesis that monkeys were capable of either imitation or reasoning.

Times have changed. The animal kingdom has experienced a "shakeup" of sorts. Monkeys, great apes, and dolphins had, for some time, been considered as the only other animals with the intelligence to be "rational." Even considering the reputed memory and learning skills of the majestic elephant, the whole lot was considered as nothing more than "apes" or "parrots," that is, imitators, not thinkers.

It doesn't take a zoologist or animal psychologist to know that animals are "smart," but do they really think? If so are there thoughts similar to ours? Do animals that evolve from earlier forms have higher levels of social intelligence? The answer would seem to be an obvious "yes!" But it goes well beyond just human-animal interaction. In an experiment with dogs and wolves, researchers found that wolves and dogs raised under the same conditions were unable to perform the impossible task of opening a container to get meat. This, needless to say, was no surprise to the research team. The dogs eventually sat, entreating their masters, while the wolves "doggedly" kept trying to open the containers—a surprise indeed! Wolves fend for themselves in the wild, but dogs don't last long under the same conditions. Interaction with humans is ingrained into the dogs' genetic code, thus turning the phrase "man's best friend" true on the biological level as well as on the social sphere. The wolves are intelligent in an environment that requires no human intervention, while the dogs are smarter on a social level with a variety of species. Dogs are good socializers but their power of logical thinking is limited.

Koko the gorilla is a wonderful example of rationality in animals, as was Alex the parrot. The African Grey parrot, which died recently, had a vocabulary of about 100 words that he combined spontaneously to answer questions and make requests. He named colors, shapes, counted objects and performed simple addition. He performed to please his trainers and audience, but when he tired of the limelight he would give every possible answer to a question except the right one, thereby frustrating his trainers with this indication that he wanted to return to his cage. Koko, a 36 year old female gorilla has mastered more than 1000 words based on American Sign Language and is able to understand approximately 2000 spoken words.

Lisa Parr of the Center for Behavioral Neuroscience at Emory University in Atlanta, Georgia, USA noted that chimpanzees' right cerebral hemispheres heat up when the chimps are exposed to scary, horror film clips and the left hemispheres warm up during happy, playful TV shows. Ms. Parr placed monitoring devices in the animals' ears to take the readings.

Self-recognition has always been a sign of intelligence, on a very basic level to be sure, but nevertheless a valid indicator. Until recently, most scientists thought that animals were unable to recognize themselves as a reflection of themselves. Diana Reiss and Lori Marino conducted a study on Presley and Tab, two of the Wildlife Conservation Society's bottlenose dolphins, to see if they could recognize themselves in a mirror. The Osborn Marine Laboratory at the New York Aquarium was the place of experimentation. Lines with odorless paint were drawn on the bodies of Tab and Presley to see if they felt the markers on their body. It turned out that the dolphins checked themselves often in the mirrors to examine their body parts they couldn't otherwise see. Reiss and Marino concluded that dolphins are the first animals other than primates to have the ability of self recognition.

Prairie dogs have a recognizable language that is as complex and diverse in many ways as is human communication. The animals can warn each other about approaching predators or just "chat" to pass the time. Con Slobodchikoff, of Northern Arizona University, who discovered the prairie dog language, claims the animals use "adjective" and "verb" chirps sometimes in full sentences. Armed with microphone and computer Slobodchikoff records the cacophony then interprets the sonogram. He can understand some chirps like "hawk" or "dog", but relies on the computer for a complete translation.

In July of 2003, a television program on the Travel Channel ranked the ten smartest animals in order of increasing intelligence as: squirrel, squid, raven, dog, pig, parrot, elephant, monkey, dolphin and ape. Do any of these animals have self-awareness? Do they think about their future or destiny? If so, do they consider themselves superior to us, inferior to us or are we their peers? These big questions must be examined so that reasonable and responsible people can eliminate cruel animal experimentation. Can we, as conscientious "human animals," make a difference in this regard. . .?

13

THE MOZART EFFECT

Links between music and human intelligence date back to the classical discoveries of Pythagoras. One of the most recent discoveries is called the "Mozart Effect."[30] A term that has been made popular in print and broadcast media, the Mozart Effect has renewed parents interest in classical music education.

Dr. Frances Rauscher and her colleagues discovered that, after listening to Mozart's sonata for two pianos in D Major K 448 for ten minutes, college students scored eight to nine points higher on spatial-temporal IQ scores than they did in periods of relaxation, instruction, or silence. The IQ-enhancing effect did not last longer than ten to fifteen minutes. Some psychologists were unable to reproduce the effect while others confirmed the IQ boost. Rauscher had stressed that the Mozart Effect was limited to spatial-temporal reasoning and that no benefits should be expected in general intelligence. An explanation for the results obtained after listening to the music may lie in the manner in which music and spatial imagery are processed within the brain. PET and functional magnetic resonance scanning have shown that listening to music activates a wide distribution of brain areas. The results of various types of tests involving spatial-temporal reasoning have shown that the prefrontal, temporal and precuneus regions of the brain are involved in music processing.

In studies of pre-schoolers, aged three to four years, it was determined that children given keyboard music lessons for six months, studying pitch intervals, fingering techniques, sight reading, musical notation and playing from memory, performed thirty percent better than other children of the same age group who were given computer lessons for six months or those who were given no specialized training. Again, the improvement was limited to spatial-temporal reasoning, and there was no effect on spatial recognition. The effect lasted unchanged for twenty-four hours, and the longer duration was attributed to the length of the exposure to the music and the elasticity of the young brain. It is generally recognized that the improvement in spatial-temporal reasoning in children after piano training accounts for their eventual higher mathematical ability.

E. Glenn Schulenberg, of the University of Toronto at Mississauga, offered Toronto-area six-year olds free weekly voice or piano lessons at the Royal Conservatory of Music. A third group of children in the study was given weekly drama lessons, while yet another group of six-year olds received no classes during the study. Before the study began, the children's IQs were tested using the full-scale Wechsler Intelligence Scale for Children (WISC). Following the test, the children began their first year of grade school and were sequestered into their various assigned groups. During a time between first and second grade, the youngsters were re-tested. All of the students showed an increase in IQ of at least 4.3 points on average. Schulenberg attributed this increase in IQ to "just going to school," nothing more. Yet an added boost to IQ scores was displayed by children taught either piano or voice. Children in these two groups had a seven-point gain in IQ from the previous year. In other words, two to seven points higher than the children placed in the drama or no-lesson groups.

The increase in IQ was small, but significant, in that the research in the Canadian study showed that the music effect ("Mozart Effect") was, according to Rauscher, valid for general intelligence and not spatial-temporal intelligence alone. Rauscher's previous work had tended to focus on spatial-temporal intelligence and exclude the possible effect of IQ enhancement to general intelligence. Rauscher is convinced that understanding music, particularly the ability to translate symbols into sound, might be transferrable to other abilities since they share similar neurological pathways. Both Rauscher and Schulenberg agree that music lessons should be available to children as a part of their school curriculum.

Dr. Gordon Shaw, a colleague of Dr. Frances Rauscher, believes that music is a window into higher brain functions. He is certain that music can help us understand how the brain works; and he shows how music may positively affect how we reason and create. In his book *Keeping Mozart in Mind,*[31] Shaw gives the reader a thorough look at over twenty-five years of his personal research on music and the brain, and includes key information from an earlier book as well as the works of other scientists.

Physician and biologist Lewis Thomas conducted a study on the undergraduate majors of medical school applicants.[32] He found that of the students who applied for medical school, those with music backgrounds were in the highest percentile of majors admitted, with a full sixty-six percent of music majors who had applied being accepted—the highest percentage of any group! In comparison, only forty-four percent of the biochemistry majors who applied were admitted. In a separate study of 7500 university students, it was revealed that music majors had the highest reading scores of all majors, including English, biology, chemistry and mathematics. A study conducted at the University of Texas[33] that looked at 362 first semester students found that music majors or those with music backgrounds were able to handle anxiety, alcohol-related problems, and were, in general, emotionally healthier than their non-musical peers. They also had more self confidence before and during examinations.

The world's top academic countries place a high value on music education, with Hungary, The Netherlands and Japan leading the way in scientific achievement. This emphasis on music education throughout the academic life of young people seems to contradict the United States' heavy focus on math, science, vocabulary and technology. It should be emphasized that this link between higher intelligence and music education is most readily observed in music making and not just passive listening. Actually, taking part is what causes the boost in brain power. Top business executives tend to agree that arts and music education programs may help repair weaknesses in school curricula and better prepare workers for the twenty-first century.

14

PERSONALITY AND CREATIVITY: EXTROVERSION VS. INTROVERSION

Social scientists believe that introversion and extroversion are basic ways of responding to our environment, produced by polygenetic influence and interaction.

According to Carl Gustav Jung (1875-1961), Swiss psychiatrist and founder of analytical psychology, an introvert is, briefly, someone who is sensitive and is continually subjecting his thoughts and actions to self-analysis and criticism. He tends to be quiet, low-key, deliberate, and disengaged from the social world. Preferring the world of fantasy and imagination, the introvert generally is a loner. Jung also coined the term "extroversion" (or "extraversion"). The extrovert, the introvert's polar opposite, is assertive, more open, places a higher value on the objective world, and generally participates in social and practical affairs instead of reverie and self-imposed solitude.

Jung referred to the libido as the general activity and drive of the individual, thus removing it from the sexual character ascribed by Sigmund Freud.[34] The control of the libido can be easily lost by the extrovert; carried beyond a "safe limit" when his feelings are acted out. Extreme introverts, on the opposite end of the scale, can succumb to fantasies that give libidinal satisfaction and have more meaning than objective reality. Severe introversion is a characteristic of autism and some forms of schizophrenia. Although all of us have tendencies in each direction, Jung did not strictly classify using the terms "introvert-extrovert."

There are advantages as well as drawbacks to both introversion and extroversion. The introvert is usually comfortable with his feelings when alone. Less noticeable than the sometimes boisterous and jolly extrovert, the introvert is not as likely to be embarrassed and criticized as is the extrovert. He has a tendency to enjoy deep, meaningful conversations and, in addition, finds it easier to meditate and is less "antsy" than his extroverted counterpart. The introvert is oftentimes more capable of keeping himself entertained, occupied, and productive than the extrovert.

Positive aspects to extroversion are the general tendency to have more friends and acquaintances than the introvert and, in studies . . .

> " . . . published in the 'Journal of Personality and Social Psychology,' William Fleeson, Ph.D., an associate professor of psychology at Wake Forest University, found that acting extroverted makes people happier (even those who are introverted at heart)".[35]

Some believe extroversion leads to personal growth, while others are certain that only through introverted and solitary practices progress is made. Creative people manipulate introversion-extroversion to grow further into their talents.

> "Of all human activities creativity comes closest to providing the fulfillment we all hope to get in our lives . . . Creativity is the central source of meaning in our lives. Most of the things that are interesting, important, and human are the result of creativity."[36]

While actively creative, the individual feels fully alive and able to adapt himself to the task of being productive in almost any situation. Creativity is a personal trait and is not necessarily a question of superior genes, rather a higher-focused mind. Creativity, itself learned through trial and error, is a strategy for achieving goals. Creative types tend to be endowed with superior intelligence, yet many psychologists believe there is a limit below which exceptional creativity is difficult, and above which a person's creativity is not significantly different from her lesser endowed peers. Most agree that IQ 120 is that magic number. Granted, those who "see further" do so because they stand upon the "shoulders of giants."[37]

Throughout history, creative geniuses have been the innovators; they are the fountain or source of modern-day art, language, and scientific/technological breakthrough.

It is difficult to determine if one is, in fact, more of an introvert or an extrovert. I recently had a telephone interview with autodidact psychometrician Dr. Greg A. Grove, a PhD in Education and a Music History professor at Santa Rosa Junior College in Northern California. Dr. Grove is the author of a test called the I-E Scale.[38] He created the I-E Scale to determine personality type (introvert—extrovert) and at the same time give the examinee an indication of his or her creativity and predicted IQ.

Dr. Grove constructed a raw-score IQ prediction scale to cover IQs 115-150. The I-E Scale is composed of twelve seemingly innocuous statements, arranged in three sections of four questions each. The examinee is told to choose the degree to which a statement applies on a scale of 0 to 5, with 0 indicating "Doesn't Apply" and 5 = "Almost Always." The I-E Scale is then self-scored and tendencies towards thinking and emotional introversion and extroversion are explained; IQ range is predicted in Table B. Of those who participated in Grove's study, the average IQ was 138.8 with the median IQ at 137.

I had heard of the test and decided to give it a go. I took the I-E Scale prior to speaking with Dr. Grove and the results compared them with other such tests that I have taken, like as the Keirsy Temperament Sorter[39] and the Jung Typology Test.[40] My general tendencies towards introversion and extroversion were, indeed, similar. The "trick" seems to be to play no tricks and answer the questions as honestly as possible.

Although introverts have been shown to have the advantage over extroverts when it comes to long-term memory and problem solving, truly creative people tend to be both extroverted and introverted, and extreme positions are rare, since most of us are ambiverts, having a balanced disposition intermediate between extroversion and introversion. The I-E Scale and the Jung Typology Test differ greatly in length. The I-E Scale asks the right questions, is brief, informative, and fun. I would suggest taking both tests to continue your journey into self-discovery. There is no fee.

15

NEURAL NETWORKS: AN OVERVIEW

The purpose of this essay is to provide the reader with a general definition of *Artificial Neural Networks*; their functioning, applications, and a few words about what the future might allow in this area.

Introduction

Artificial neural networks are emulations patterned after the most sophisticated and powerful problem-solving device ever created, the human brain: a vast network of processing elements and nerve cells. The concept of neural networks dates back to the 1800s and is an attempt to describe how the human mind performs. The human brain is still largely an unsolved mystery; much is still unknown about how the brain trains itself and processes information. The human brain has been a source of inspiration for *Artificial Intelligence* since the dawn of the computer age. With the advance of modern neuroimaging[41] techniques, we can look into the brain of a human being and measure its activity.

Human Neural Network

A *Human Neural Network* is an interconnected system of neurons in the brain or other parts of the body. In the human brain, a neuron collects signals from other neurons (brain cells, mostly) through a host of fine structures known as *dendrites*.[42] The neuron sends out spikes of electricity through a long, thin strand called an *axon*,[43] which splits into thousands of branches. At the end of each branch, there is a *synapse,*[44] which converts the activity from the axon into electrical effects and inhibits or excites activity from the axon which, in turn, inhibits or excites electrical activity in the connected neurons. When a neuron receives stimuli that are sufficiently large, compared to its inhibitory input, it sends a spike of electrical activity down the axon. Learning occurs by changing the effectiveness of the synapses so that one neuron's influence affects another neuron.

Diagram 1: Human Neural Network

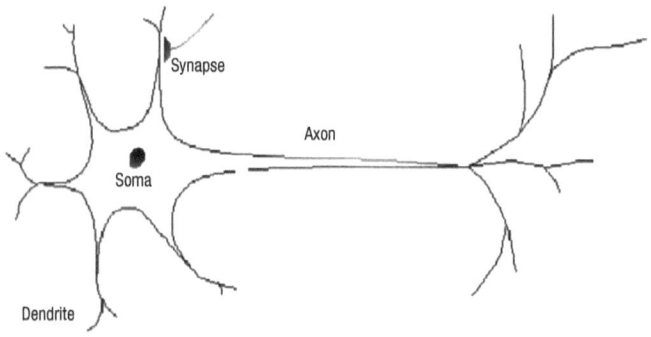

Computer scientists began analyzing these ideas with the Turing B-type[45] machines and the Perceptron[46] in the 1950s. Friedrich Hayek[47] postulated the idea of spontaneous order in the brain arising out of decentralized networks known as neurons. By 1975, the Cognitron[48] had made its appearance. Hopfield's[49] Network had the ability for bidirectional flow of inputs between neurons and nodes; and the specialization of these node layers was introduced through the first hybrid network. In the mid-1980s, "Parallel Distributed Processing"[50] became widely known as "Connectivism."[51] A report entitled *Learning Internal Representation by Error Propagation*[52] was one of the main reasons behind the re-popularization of neural networks. The original network used multiple layers of weight-sum units of the type f = g(w' x+b) where "g" was a sigmoid function (or a function used in "Logistic Regression").[53] The employment of the chain rule of differentiation in deriving the appropriate parameter update results in an algorithm that appears to back propagate errors; hence, the name. Networks with the same architecture are now referred to as "Multilayer Perceptrons."[54]

Artificial Neural Networks (ANNs)

Artificial Neural Networks try to simulate the structure and functional aspects of biological neural networks. ANNs have very high processing speeds, and they have the ability to learn how to solve a problem from a given set of examples. These characteristics afford us a variety of powerful new techniques for solving certain problems. In the same way that a human being becomes an expert in a specific area, computer scientists train neural networks in a given area. Once automatic learning has been established, a neural network learns on its own through practice and repeated experience. When it has been proven that the neural network is doing its job correctly, it has become an "expert" and operates according to its own decisions and judgments. As has been indicated, a human neural network is a circuit of biological neurons. However, the term "Neural Network" often refers to an Artificial Neural Network, composed of artificial neurons or nodes. Artificial Neural Network (ANN), Simplified Neural Network (SNN), or, simply, Neural Network (NN), are terms that refer to the same idea. While many types of artificial neural networks exist, most are organized according to the same basic structure:

Diagram 2: Artificial Neural Network

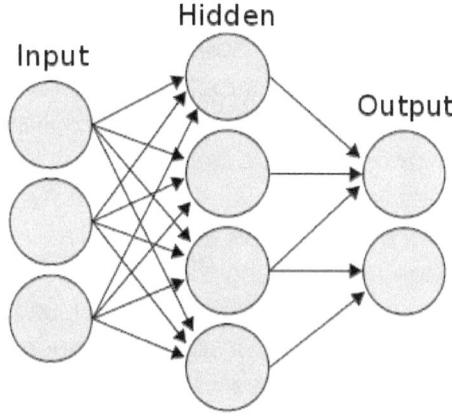

An Artificial neural network is a processing paradigm that can recognize patterns in a given collection of data and produce a model for that data. It resembles the brain in two respects: Knowledge is acquired by the network through a trial-and-error learning process. Interneuron connection strengths ("synaptic weights") are used to store the knowledge.

Artificial neural networks are an emulation of human brain function. They are made with hardware and software with the purpose of ratiocination, learning, following patterns and predicting, while processing an elevated number of elements or variables which are interconnected. Artificial neural networks commonly use mathematical models, diffuse logic, Bayesian inference,[55] Fourier Transforms[56] and Expert Systems.[57]

Thomas J Hally

How do Neural Networks Function?

Conventional computers use a cognitive, algorithmic approach to problem solving. That is, they follow a set of programmed instructions to solve a problem. This approach restricts the problem-solving capability of conventional computers, since it is a problem we already know and understand how to solve. The computer's instructions are converted into a high-level language program and then into machine code or low-level language (e.g., Assembly Language) that the computer understands. Since the computer is totally predictable, if anything goes wrong it is due to a software or hardware problem.

The key element of the paradigm is the novel structure of the information processing system, which is composed of a large number of neurons working in union to solve specific problems. An ANN configured for a special application (e.g., pattern recognition and data classification) has gone through a learning process. Like humans, ANNs learn with biological adjustments to the synaptic connections that exist between neurons. Artificial intelligence and cognitive modeling try to assimilate some properties of neural networks and have been applied successfully to speech recognition, image analysis and adaptive control. This assimilation has as its objectives the construction of software agents in both video games and autonomous robots. Most of the currently employed neural networks for artificial intelligence are based on Statistical Estimation,[58] Optimization,[59] and Control Theory.[60]

Since ANNs process information in a similar way to the way the human brain, they learn by example. Learning comes about by changing the effectiveness of the synapses so that the influence of neurons on one another changes. Neural networks cannot be programmed to perform a specific task. The examples or problems must be carefully selected so that time is not wasted. The disadvantage is that its learning capability finds out how to solve the problem by itself and the operation can be unpredictable.

Artificial neural networks and conventional computers complement each other. There are tasks more suited to an algorithmic approach—like arithmetic operations—and tasks that are more suitable for neural networks (e.g., "classification"). The latter includes pattern and sequence recognition as well as a plethora of distinct novelty detections and sequential decision-making procedures. Moreover, a large number of tasks require combinations of these two systems. Normally, a conventional computer is used to oversee the neural network; both the conventional computer and the neural network perform at top efficiency when used in conjunction. The neural network functions within the scheme of any number of computer arrays:

Diagram 3: Artificial Neural Network using a Computer Algorithm

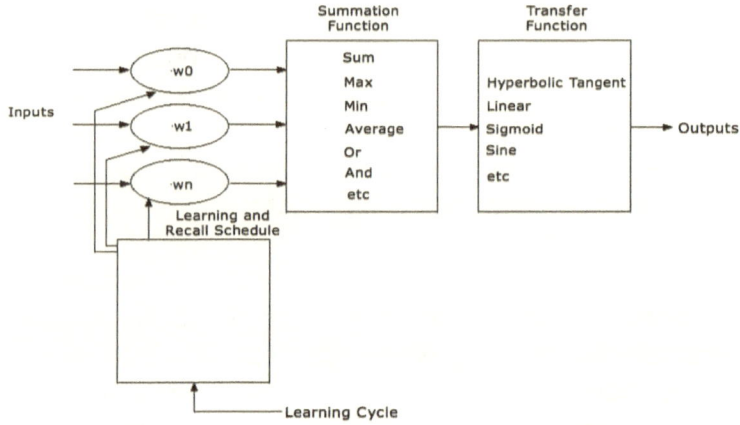

Train the Neural Network

- Present data to the network.
- Network produces an output.
- Network output compared to a desired output.
- Network strengths are modified to reduce error.

An artificial neural network can perform tasks that a linear program cannot. When any given element of a neural network fails, the ANN can continue without incident because of its parallel nature. The neural network learns and does not need to be reprogrammed. It can be implemented in almost any application, and this can be done without any problem.

Typical ANN Applications

The tasks to which ANNs are applied tend to fall within three categories, mostly in business and medicine:

1. Function approximation or regression analysis.
2. Classification, including pattern recognition and sequence recognition.
3. Data processing.

Most practical applications of artificial neural networks are based on a computational model involving the propagation of continuous variables from one processing to the next. In recent years, data from neurobiological experiments have made increasingly clear that biological neural networks, which communicate through pulses, use the timing of these pulses to transmit information and perform computation. This realization has stimulated significant research on pulsed neural networks, including theoretical analyses and model development, neurobiological modeling, and hardware implementation.[61]

Classification
- Medical diagnoses, fraud detection, character recognition, speech recognition, etc.

Function Approximation
Process modeling
- Data processing, filtering, clustering, compression, etc.

Process control
- Data modeling, machine diagnostics.

Time Series Prediction
- Financial forecasting, bankruptcy, prediction sales, forecasting Dynamic System Marketing.

Data Mining Clustering
- Data recognition, data extraction.

What does the Future hold for Artificial Neural Networks?

"The applications are very diverse, from climactic predictions to autonomous prostheses."[62] The following are but a few examples of what computer scientists have planned for humankind's future:

1. Robots that can see, feel, and predict the world around them.
2. Improved stock prediction.
3. Common usage of self-driving cars.
4. Composition of music.
5. Handwritten documents to be automatically transformed and formatted into word-processing documents.
6. Trends found in the human genome to aid in the Human Genome Project.
7. Self-diagnosis of medical problems using artificial neural networks.

Conclusion

A common criticism of neural networks is that they require a large diversity of training to perform practical operations. This is particularly true in robotics. Other criticisms come from advocates of "hybrid models," those combining neural networks and symbolic approaches. These critics support the combination of these two approaches, believing that hybrids can better emulate the mechanisms of the human mind. Yet, artificial neural networks are destined to play an important role in medicine, psychology (including the study of human cognitive ability), robotics, and nanotechnology. Neural networking promises to provide computer science breakthroughs that rival anything we have yet witnessed. Once neural networks are properly trained, they can replace many human functions in targeted areas.

Perhaps the most exciting possibility is that of "conscious" neural networks. However, neural network consciousness will always be an alien consciousness. I seriously doubt there will ever be an artificial neural network that will superintend its creators. Artificial neural networks will never feel, think, or perceive as we do, much less ponder their own destinies.

16

DOES OUR CREATIVITY DECLINE AS WE GROW OLDER?

When we were youngsters our minds were open to new and fantastic possibilities. Our burgeoning curiosity guided us through primeval forests of adventure and discovery. Always investigating life and our surroundings, we queried our parents and older siblings and searched within ourselves and the totality of nature for the answers to our questions. So what happens to this adventurous, inquisitive spirit of ours when we get older? Do we lose our child-like wonderment? The answer is a tentative *yes* and *no*.

The decline in creativity does not necessarily start when we reach the age of 40 or 50. This process can begin when we first enter school. At about four and five years of age, we are using a huge percentage of our potential. We are discovering and inventing: we are *creating*. It does not matter if what we are creating was created before because we have no knowledge of it other than our own experience. We innovate at a remarkable pace; yet, by the onset of puberty, at about 12 years old, it is not unusual for many of us to have quashed our creative spirit considerably. This can and does happen, and some of us are "doomed" to stay in that rut for the rest of our lives.

Conformity is the price we pay to live in a modern world. To get along with our peers and our superiors, we must follow a set of rules and adopt values. Life seems to be more about what we *cannot* do than what we *can* do. We have—long ago, it seems—stopped inventing our world and we are doing what others tell us we must do. Our once childlike curiosity has transmogrified into predictable behavior and the rote memorization of facts and rules.

Creativity can be threatening to those who have been conditioned to conformity, and, in order to "get along" and not "rock the boat," we tend to stifle our creative energy. Starting in our elementary school years, conformity is drilled into us; hence our ability to creatively solve problems suffers. We learn there is only one way to solve them: the way our teacher has in mind. This teacher is the same person who learned these same rules of conformity, adapted to the current mores, when he or she, too, was an elementary school student. The cycle repeats itself, generation after generation. By the time we reach college, we have been thoroughly conditioned to pay heed to every syllable our professors utter as if they were proclaiming the ineluctable "Word of God." We are indeed functional members of society when we graduate—but we may also be no more creative than robots![63]

Cognitive traps[64] and illness are the primary reasons for fading creativity in elderly people. Happily, *maturity* offers us an opportunity to resoundingly defeat the "humdrum monotony" that is our daily routine. Even if we are older, within each of us there still exists the world of our childhood: the fantastic, the improbable, and the surreal faces of self-discovery and self-surrender. We must reach within ourselves and yield to this special inner world in order to unfold to our full potential. Let us remember, if we dare, those things that captured our imaginations as youngsters and adolescents; those early phases of our life that captivated us—besides our teenage obsessions with opposite sex! Once again, we test our abilities and cultivate our gardens: we have a knack for writing poetry and fiction: let this natural resource blossom. Looking back to our youthful years, we consider our long-ago-abandoned hobbies. They will guide us through waters we had hitherto considered impossible to navigate.[65]

Remember, locking ourselves into a repetitive, boring routine can only make us *less* creative. We must use our intelligence and creativity to enrich the lives of others as well as our own, whether we are young or old.[66]

Fluid intelligence (*Gf*) tends to decrease as we age, and mild short-term memory loss is considered normal; yet, our vast reservoir of crystallized intelligence (*Gc*) does not decline.[67] Theories of a universal decline in creativity and intelligence linked to "the inevitable consequence of aging" are patently false:

> "Among the mentally alert and healthy elderly, recent cognitive studies have shown that intelligence among the aged does not inevitably decline," said Harry R. Moody, deputy director of the Brookdale Center. "In some areas," Dr. Moody said, "as in tests measuring insight into problem situations, in creative understanding, and metaphoric processing, older people show actual statistical gains" . . . To Marc Kaminsky, director and creator of the two-year-old Artists and Elders Project, "The life-review process is the cutting edge where gerontology and the humanities meet. Old people's reminiscences can be shaped in the form of journals, poetry, novels and plays. They can create works of power that have meaning to themselves, and great resonance in society."[68]

If we start to do different things, such as going to new places; talking with people we have recently befriended; reading a variety of books and newspapers; studying a foreign language on our own—or even returning to school late in life with the eventual goal of completing a bachelor's or graduate degree—we cannot help but synergize and synthesize and regenerate our generative powers. A cornucopia of possibilities awaits us.

Healthy, creative people normally outlive those who do not have a modicum of creativity in their lifestyles. All other things being equal, intellectually active individuals can live as long as those who stay in tip-top physical condition.[69,70]

Just use it!

17

IQ, INTELLIGENCE, ETHNICITY AND GENDER

Mainstream concepts and studies of IQ and intelligence attempt to explain the nature, origins and practical consequences of individual and group intelligence. The problem with these explorations into the human intellectual machine is that they are generally biased and stereotyped, depending upon a model which is culturally incomprehensible to many Third World people, Africans in particular.

In a statement signed by Raymond B. Cattell, Hans Eysenck, Arthur R. Jensen and Richard Lynn, all eminent professors and experts in the field of intelligence and IQ testing, they concur that the definition of intelligence is "general mental capacity that involves the ability to reason, solve problems, think abstractly, comprehend complex ideas, learn quickly and learn from experience." These gentlemen agree that intelligence is not merely book learning or test-taking smarts; rather it reflects a broader and deeper capability for comprehending one's surroundings. It is important to realize that "catching on," "making sense" and "figuring out" are the key factors in "intelligence." The professors also agree that IQ tests measure this general ability, and that most standardized IQ tests measure more or less the same traits. (So far so good!)

However, they overemphasize the role genetic factors play in the measurement and understanding of human intelligence. According to these men and forty-eight other signees who approve the conclusions of the book *The Bell Curve*,[71] Blacks are doomed to be less intelligent than Whites and Asians. The group further declares that there is no convincing evidence that the IQ bell curves for different racial groups are converging. In unison they affirm that there is no definite answer as to why IQ bell curves differ across racial-ethnic groups.

Could it be that IQ tests themselves hold the key to this problem? Is it really *genetics* that explains why a hungry school-age child in a desert in Ethiopia or student in some war-torn area of the globe does not learn math and language as well or score as high on an IQ test as his counterpart living in a middle-class neighborhood in the self-proclaimed "First World"? Is genetics the *only* answer why the latter child is at peace with himself and his environment and has the benefit of a decent education and parents who can care for him? The signees believe that research on matters of intelligence relate to some *unclear* social and, primarily, *biological* distinctions.

A phenomenon known as the Flynn Effect[72] may reduce or eliminate differences in IQ between races and cultures in the future. With IQ scores in affluent Holland and Spain up by six to eight points respectively in just one decade—and an astonishing twenty-six point increase in the past fourteen years in developing Kenya—it is evident that the Flynn Effect is a reality and that genetic bias against Blacks is meaningless. There is, in addition, an argument that the average IQ in the United States was a mere 75 before improved nutrition increased the scores of the general population.[73] The IQ for the average American is currently 98.

It is almost universally agreed upon that a person's IQ can predict academic success, but not how to function successfully in one's environment. Furthermore, there is considerable evidence from re-testing and the application of different tests that a person's IQ *does not remain fixed* during his lifetime. Emotional and motivational factors play a key role on how one scores on any given test and may vary from one test to another. It is a believed that as many as sixty percent of IQ test scores change significantly over time. With this in mind, can we properly assume that a test score accessed at a particular point in an individual's life is a valid indicator of his *native* intelligence?

G ("general intelligence") is as controversial as it is cultural. The core element in measuring a person's intelligence is *vocabulary*. Vocabulary reflects one's cognitive skills, and exposure to words is not genetic; it is learned. A child or an adult who has never seen an octagon or the male icon or symbol (♂) or the icon symbol for female (♀) would certainly not recognize them if they were presented to him in an intelligence test. The genetic component in IQ is the reciprocal of the environmental component: the larger the difference in environments, the less the component determined by genes will appear.

Today, it is acceptable and realistic to embrace the view that racial and gender differences are not genetic but reflect social and environmental challenges.

Consider, if you will, Harvard University's former President Lawrence Summers' commencement address on January 14, 2005. Here is an excerpt:

> I'm going to confine myself to addressing one portion of the problem, or of the challenge we're discussing, which is the issue of women's representation in tenured positions in science and engineering at top universities and research institutions, not because that's necessarily the most important problem or the most interesting problem, but because it's the only one of these problems that I've made an effort to think in a very serious way about. The other prefatory comment that I would make is that I am going to, until most of the way

through, attempt to adopt an entirely positive, rather than normative approach, and just try to think about and offer some hypotheses as to why we observe what we observe without seeing this through the kind of judgmental tendency that inevitably is connected with all our common goals of equality. It is after all not the case that the role of women in science is the only example of a group that is significantly underrepresented in an important activity and whose underrepresentation contributes to a shortage of role models for others who are considering being in that group. To take a set of diverse examples, the data will, I am confident, reveal that Catholics are substantially underrepresented in investment banking, which is an enormously high-paying profession in our society; that white men are very substantially underrepresented in the National Basketball Association; and that Jews are very substantially underrepresented in farming and in agriculture. These are all phenomena in which one observes underrepresentation, and I think it's important to try to think systematically and clinically about the reasons for underrepresentation.[74]

After his speech, *some concluded* that Summers intimated that gender differences in intrinsic ability were a cause of the dearth of top echelon female scientists, and that he "cavalierly disregarded" the realities of bias in hiring, discriminatory tenure practices and negative stereotypes. With the unabated furor over his remarks suggesting that women may not have the same innate abilities in math and science as men, Harvard's president, Lawrence H. Summers, issued a two-page apology to the Harvard community, saying he was wrong to have spoken in a way that resulted in an unintended signal of discouragement to talented girls and women. Summers's letter was posted on his Harvard Web site. After a flurry of controversy, Lawrence Summers resigned.

Phillip Emeagwali, who helped give a boost to the supercomputer, is a Nigerian-born scientist who stunned the world of high tech and high IQ when he won the Gordon Bell Prize in 1989. The fact that a Black African would have an IQ of 190 and be married to a Black American microbiologist and biochemist may have caused racist Nobel Prize-winner Dr. William Shockley to roll over in his grave.[75] Ironically, Shockley died the same year that Emeagwali won the Gordon Bell Prize for The Connection Machine.[76]

Andy Warhol was one of the most important representatives of pop art and best remembered for his representations of Campbell's Soup cans. Warhol created hundreds of other works during his allotted 58 years, including commercial advertisements, films, the blotted-line technique and the process of silk screening in painting. His IQ was, allegedly, a mere 86. Yet many would call *both* Emeagwali and Warhol geniuses despite the 104 point difference in IQ scores.[77]

The idea that one homogeneous group of people is necessarily smarter than (or dumber than) another such group should be discarded. Clearly there will always be individual differences, but it should be emphasized that *any* adaptable individual who possesses sufficient ability and motivation will most likely be a success in his elected vocation.

18

RIGHT BRAIN/LEFT BRAIN: ONE OR TWO—OR THREE?

Concepts of the duality of human nature, such as Yin and Yang have been hypotheses of philosophers and scientists from time immemorial. Humans have been preoccupied with their intelligence in the practical sense since the days of the first troglodytes, and in aesthetic and theoretical sense since a Cro-Magnon artist painted a bison on the wall of Altamira Cave, near Santander, Spain.

A brief synopsis of popular definitions of intelligence is in order. When someone says "She is intelligent" what they usually mean is that "she agrees with me." This is the definition most people are comfortable with.

There are other, more reliable definitions of intelligence, needless to say, and here are just a few: Benet and Simon (1916) defined intelligence as the ability to "to judge well, to reason well, and to comprehend well." By 1921 Louis Terman had come up with a concept of intelligence as "the ability to carry out abstract thinking," and Freeman, thirty plus years later, sized up intelligence as "the extent to which a person is educable." A more recent reference to intelligence includes Wechsler (1975) who defined intelligence from the computer scientists' point of view as "the ability to process information" and from the psychologists' vista as "the ability to deduce relationships" while educators saw intelligence as "the ability to learn." More basic still was the biologists' definition as "the ability to adapt to the environment." Well, one thing is certain, the more of these abilities we are equipped with, the better off we are.

We are all endowed with one brain—or is it really two? The right controls the left and the left controls the right. This is how our brain and body function together. The right brain is creative, spiritual and emotional, while the left brain analyzes and judges. The cerebrum, the seat of complex thought, is divided into two hemispheres. Each hemisphere of the brain is dominant for its behaviors, and most of us tend to favor one style of thinking. Our choices in life depend on a particular dominance; and it is generally believed that highly creative people are right brain dominant, while most scientists and mathematicians are considered left brain dominant.

Lefties *were* considered "smarter" than righties. Left brains tend to be objective, logical, analytical, and sequential, generally favoring careers such as law, accounting and science. They tend to be skeptical of anything new and untried; and many are also likely to eschew traditional religious beliefs. Most are lovers of classical music and are not as apt as righties (who favor rock and roll) at "thinking outside the box." When a left brain does come up with something innovative, it is likely that it is an original idea of a right brain. The left brain individual might not have been prone to create whatever it was in the first place. The left, "academic brain," sees the components of the picture.

Rights think in visual, kinesthetic and audio images. Abstract math is often not brain compatible. Right brains process information in a random manner, going from point A to point D without the necessity to read a detailed list of instructions, getting the whole picture in one quick scan. They are seen as non-judgmental and often have no opinion on many topics. The right brain mode is the holistic mode, incorporating intuitive and non-verbal functioning. A bilateral transfer is achieved by an unconscious process shared with the left hemisphere and the corpus callosum, the arched bridged of nerve tissues that connects the two. Full consciousness arises from the collaboration of the two sets of processes. The four active parts in the right brain/left brain hemispheres are the frontal lobe, which controls personality, the temporal lobe, dealing with long and short term memory, the parietal lobe which maneuvers the hands, while the occipital lobe guides our vision. The right, "artistic brain," is global, seeing the whole picture.

In the left brain dominant, emotions become a symbolic memory ("I was happy/sad yesterday") and not a feeling sensation of the actual experience. When a person is in a right brain mode of emotional turbulence, such as rage, grief—or even love—he or she is often left speechless. How did we become such a bundle of confusion? Left brain dominance probably came about as a result of the basic need to survive in a primitive and physical world, from food gathering to killing as a survival tactic. To do this man had to turn off feelings that would prohibit killing of animals and fellow humans. We had to sacrifice for the good of society, which meant organizing in larger groups and giving up our autonomy. The right brain (awareness) takes those facts developed by the left brain (consciousness), and makes the proper connections from them, in turn making things meaningful. Again, this is achieved through bi-lateral transfer. And there is now considered to be a third brain, "kinesthetic thought," a combination of the verbal and visual together. Both sides of the brain can interchange rules. This is part of the "whole brain" pattern.

It would be interesting to see what percentage of Mensans is left brain dominant and what percentage fits the "right" pattern. My opinion is that there are more whole-brained members of our society than the strictly right and left varieties combined. Just a guess . . .

19

WHAT IS WI-FI AND HOW DOES IT WORK?

Recently, I purchased a Dell Vostro 1500 laptop to add to my collection that consists of an old Gateway 5200S desktop, an iPad3, and a super-duper HP Pavilion dv6, a too-many-Gigabytes-to-remember laptop. I decided to set up a local area network (LAN) in my home since all of my computers are equipped with Wi-Fi (or the 802.11 Standard).

So what exactly *is* Wi-Fi? The simplest answer is that Wi-Fi is a high-speed, wireless Internet connection. Wireless is the key word. A computer that has Wi-Fi capability does not need wires or phone plugs to function. Wi-Fi uses radio waves like cell phones do. When you have the necessary hardware in your computer you can connect to the Internet with a simple left click of your mouse. The hardware in your computer converts data to be sent into radio waves, which, in turn, are sent to the Internet and from there on to a router to be decoded. Wi-Fi-equipped computers operate with speeds of 2.4GHz and 5GHz. Thus your computer's frequency is much faster than your cell phone's. Wi-Fi captures radio waves and transmits them by means of an antenna. A wireless router receives the signal and sends it on to the router to be decoded. The router sends the data (in binary: 1, 0) to the Internet via the Ethernet. This process is carried out in the same logical manner when the router receives information from the Internet. The router receives information from the Internet and it is decoded by the router which sends the data to a wireless adapter.

Wi-Fi facilitates applications of wireless networks such as wide area networks (WANs) in vehicles or technology that allows you to switch from a particular wireless network to another without difficulty. Wi-Fi can transmit using as much as three bands simultaneously. Wi-Fi can also hop from one frequency to another without any problems. "Frequency hopping" is very convenient since it allows multiple devices (computers, television, cell phones, etc.) quick access to the same wireless connection simultaneously.

Creating a Wireless Network

If you are thinking of building a wireless network in your home, the first thing you must consider is to insure your computer has the correct speed. Fortunately, most new laptops and many desktops are built with wireless transmitters. If you happen to have a computer without Wi-Fi you can purchase a wireless adapter that plugs into the PC Card or in a USB port.

Let's assume you are a "technology geek" like me and have three, four—or more—computers but not all of your machines have Wi-Fi. In order to turn your computer into a Wi-Fi "hotspot" you must use a wireless adaptor. Once you have installed your wireless adaptor your computer will automatically discover existing networks. Connecting to public hotspots is very convenient.

If you want to replace that tired old Ethernet network, purchase a wireless router. A wireless router contains the following: 1) a port to connect to the modem (DSL); 2) a router; 3) an Ethernet hub; 4) a firewall; and, 5) a wireless access point. The wireless router allows you to use wireless signals in order to connect a computer to others.

Routers used in the home or business can cover up to 100 feet (or 30.5 meters). A large home may need repeaters for extension. Like wireless adaptors, many routers can use more than one Wi-Fi or 802.11 Standard. 802.11b routers are a bit less expensive than 802.11, but because the standard is older, they are slower than 802.11a, 802.11g, and 802.11n routers. Most people opt for 802.11g because it is faster and more reliable than the others.

Security is a very import factor when you consider creating your own wireless local area network (LAN) in your home or business. The same holds true for public Wi-Fi in hospitals, coffee shops, and airports, etc. You should configure your router to create a hotspot—your own local area network. Your network may be vulnerable to an alert hacker. Anyone who has a wireless card, whether a guest in your home or a client, will be able to use your signal. Therefore, you should take a few precautionary steps: Make sure your security measures are up to date. There are, in addition, other steps you should take to keep your network private: 1) Wi-Fi Protected Access is part of the 802.11 wireless network security protocol. WPA provides security for your signature and password. Most public hotspots use WPA technology. 2) MAC or Media Access Control is a bit different from WPA. MAC works in conjunction with your computer's hardware. Each computer has its own unique MAC. When using MAC you must specify addresses allowed in your wireless network when you set up your router. MAC is very safe yet it is not 100 percent foolproof. Skilled hackers can fool MAC and copy an address and use it to get into your wireless LAN. Wireless networks are fast, safe (when security is in place), reliable, and inexpensive.

Good luck setting up your own wireless network!

20

THE UPS AND DOWNS OF
EMOTIONAL INTELLIGENCE

Would you believe someone who told you that his IQ was 160, and his EQ was 90? In a hospital psychiatric ward situation you just might, but in the outside world it is a fairly uncommon situation, except of course in Hi-IQland. Emotional intelligence usually correlates closely with academic intelligence, but there are notable exceptions to this rule.

In 1920, E.L. Thorndike used the term "social intelligence" to describe the skill of getting along well with other people, but the term "emotional intelligence" seems to have originated with Charles Darwin in 1872;

he more broadly applied it to survival and adaptation in humans, which is, in that sense, social intelligence.

Briefly, emotional intelligence can be viewed as the ability to understand, perceive and manage one's feelings and the ability to perceive and understand the feelings of one's fellow humans. Psychologist Daniel Goleman popularized the term in 1995, and published books and articles about the application of emotional intelligence to business. Being endowed with a good memory and good problem-solving abilities does not mean that one has the capability of dealing with his emotions or is self-motivated. Sometimes the social skills necessary to "get along" must be acquired in later years, after a child has reached his or her maturity. This is particularly true of people with Asperger's syndrome, or the highly creative schizophrenic and the bi-polar adult.

In Goleman's book, *When Smart is Dumb: Why it can matter more than IQ*, he cites examples of high IQ'ers who are not high achievers. He emphasizes that academic intelligence has little to do with emotional life . . . people with high IQs can be stunningly poor pilots of their private lives. Goleman shows how the traditionally successful person is one who deals with his emotions within the norm and mores of his culture. He defines success in social terms in a narrow way that may or may not be acceptable to the gifted person. A gifted individual is undoubtedly apt at learning a list of socially acceptable rules and reactions, but authority figures in the lives of the gifted child or adult are repeatedly challenged. Having examined the list of acceptable behaviors and rules, the gifted person often decides they are unjust or wrong. But these rules are old, self-reinforcing, and resistant to change. The gifted person must learn to adopt to his or her environment if he or she expects to ("somehow") belong.

It is nevertheless essential that a gifted child learns to "fit in." It may sometimes be the traditional bitter pill to swallow if done later in life for some of the artistically inclined and the creative poet, the writer, or those who thrive in a topsy-turvy state of mind or mood. It seems that when they are sad they are happy, and when they are manic they are productive. The acceptance of John Forbes Nash's eccentricities enabled the 1994 Nobel Prize winning economist and mathematician to leave medications behind, despite his paranoid schizophrenia. He thrives. One in an almost similar mental situation as Nash, but not so lucky, was impressionist painter, Vincent van Gough. Beat Generation author and poet Jack Kerouac was too emotionally impaired to lead a "normal life." But he most certainly made his mark in life. Was he a failure because of low emotional intelligence or was he a "howling" success like his friend, poet Alan Ginsberg?[78]

Moderate to high emotional intelligence facilitates good choices, defers gratification, helps achieve long-term goals and aids in effective relations with one's fellow employees or employer. Those with low emotional intelligence are at risk of social problems, regardless of IQ. They tend to eschew social gatherings like parties and outings. They are ill-equipped for such close person to person contact with "normals" that are not able to tolerate their weirdness or erratic behavior. Social skills can be learned at any age. On the extreme right side of the Gaussian Curve, those youngsters with very high levels of emotional intelligence sometimes feel overwhelmed by their emotions and the complexities of managing their feelings. These children, will probably not develop into emotionally mature adults without close parental guidance or counseling, though the odds are better for them than for the low EI children.

There are various EQ tests on the Internet. Those Mensans whose EQ closely correlates with their IQ should congratulate themselves and then make a hefty contribution to the mental health organization of their choice. It couldn't hurt!

21

"DIVINE MADNESS"

Three years ago, I wrote an article for the *Mensa International Journal* entitled *Creative Genius or Psychotic?* This current paper is an attempt to fill in a few glaring empty spots in my original article by including some important and relevant information. I have learned a great deal in my research on creativity and concepts of intelligence during my ongoing tenure as a writer for the MIJ and the IJ Extra, and it is my pleasure to share a bit of what I have learned with you.

Many are interested in the link between "madness" and creativity. It is widely-held belief in scientific circles that creative people have low levels of *latent inhibition*, or, as it is frequently defined, *an animal's unconscious ability to ignore stimuli that experience has shown to be irrelevant to its needs.* (Change "animal" to "human" in the previous sentence and you have it in a nutshell.) Low latent inhibition is as essential to the creative individual as is fantasy proneness. Indeed, low latent inhibition is a key factor in defining the creative individual. Those afflicted with any one of several types of mental disorders are probably also prone to fantasy and possess low levels of latent inhibition.

Could there be a biological basis for creativity linked to mental illness? Low latent inhibition and fantasy proneness are two traits psychotic individuals have in common with creative individuals. And they go hand in hand with each other. Low latent inhibition, a certain degree of intelligence, and fantasy proneness all factor into a theory of how creativity and psychoses are intertwined. Psychologists at the University of Toronto and Harvard University have identified one of the biological bases of creativity. They contend that the brains of creative people are more open to incoming stimuli from the surrounding environment than are their non-creative counterparts. The non-creative individuals may shut out this same information by means of high levels of latent inhibition.

The University of Toronto-Harvard University research teams have also shown that, by means of psychological testing, creative individuals had low levels of latent inhibition while the non-creative subjects in the study showed high levels of latent inhibition. Hence, the creative subjects were more in tune to external stimuli and used the extra information from their environment constantly. According to psychology professor Jordan Peterson of the University of Toronto, "The normal person classifies an object, and then forgets about it, even though the object is much more complex and interesting than he or she thinks. The creative person, by contrast, is always open to new possibilities."

Some researchers concur that the link between genius and a small percentage of schizophrenics "boils down" to a particular gene called DARPP-32: dopamine and cyclic AMP-regulated phosphoprotein, which works as a neurotransmitter and links genius to madness. Three quarters of any given population inherit a version of the DARPP-32 gene which enhances the brain's thinking activity by improving the information processing of the prefrontal cortex. It orchestrates thoughts and actions. Doctor Daniel Weinberger of the United States Institute for Mental Health believes the DARPP-32 gene translates into a hindrance during a severe schizophrenic episode. Creativity may "backfire," bringing tragic consequences.

Sylvia Plath was a gifted bipolar poet who had a "topsy-turvy" life. It was cut short in 1963 when she ended it. She was 30 years old. Vincent van Gogh committed suicide at the age of 37. It is speculated that he, too, was bipolar. Former British Prime Minister Winston Churchill was also a manic-depressive. Both Beat-Generation poet Jack Kerouac and economist/ mathematician and Nobel Prize winner John Forbes Nash fall into the schizophrenic diagnostic.

Mild mania and hallucinations can engender original thought processes and can even elevate one's IQ score. Auditory and visual hallucinations are symptoms of fantasy-prone people in general and not only schizophrenics and manic depressives. Paranoia, in a mild form, and moderate depression operate as "checks" to excesses in thought and action. They can also be powerful tools in bringing an individual to a high level of creative accomplishment.

The Classical Greeks believed that creative inspiration ("afflatus") was achieved through altered states of the mind. This creative inspiration is commonly called "Divine Madness." Creative minds and some pathological minds seem to follow the same cognitive pattern.

When very high intelligence, fantasy proneness and low latent inhibition coalesce in one individual— *voilà*, a creative genius is born.

22

ROBOTIC CONSCIOUSNESS

One of the philosophical and scientific problems concerning the evolution of robots is *consciousness.* Human beings are complex, self-controlling, self-sustaining machines which have been "designed" through natural selection. So why would that make us like robots? Simply put, robots are designed with many of these same characteristics.

The Hard Problem, proposed by David Chalmers, refers to the scientific problem of consciousness, the understanding of how physical processes in the brain relate to the subjective experience. *The Less Hard Problems,* but by no means easy, relate to the functions of consciousness in perception, cognition, and behavior in humans and animals, the environment of evolutionary adaptedness (EEA). These functions are necessary for the "lifestyles" of autonomous robots since functional consciousness and physical motion are integral parts of their machinery. And just as humans must have deliberate control of their actions, autonomous robots need that ability while they are operating under exceptional circumstances, such as learning new skills. In both "species" this control becomes automatic once it is learned. It is the integration from memory and various sensory modalities, such as the visual and kinesthetic. This is within the *domain of consciousness awareness. Visual dominance* might be a good place for the integration of information in artificial consciousness since it permits detailed imaging of remote objects and the robotic "understanding" of these objects, and thus proper instruction with them. Robotic self-awareness is awareness of itself as a physical object in a physical environment, not in an environment with the full ontological considerations and metaphysical premises which humans generally consider. *Metacognition* requires the reasoning about and behind one's actions and the need for understanding of behavior by deliberating these actions and their consequences. This would actually attribute *ego consciousness* to a machine! Incredible as it may seem, this is the scenario. An autonomous robot must possess lower-level or discursive reasoning as well as analog simulation via neuronal "mirror cells" to understand behavior. This uniqueness in the machines' learning to communicate with each other is meaningful to the robots; and it is meaningful to man inasmuch he is the designer of these marvels.

Briefly, the *Chinese Room Experiment* refers to a subject (computer) who knows nothing of the Chinese language but speaks Chinese through the memorization of phrases. The computer would not be able to point out a dog when asked to do so in that language, nor would it (the human inside the computer) be able to draw a picture of a dog. Nothing would be understood by the speaker about which they were speaking. Computers are not conscious in the customary sense, but as we come to understand neuronal mechanisms implementing functional consciousness, we may begin to apply them to robotic design so that autonomous robots can benefit from them as well, demonstrating functional consciousness similar to—yet far different from—human consciousness. The Chinese Room Experiment helps us to understand the difference between consciousness and *intentionality.* Although robots exhibit intrinsic intentionality, they will never be "conscious" or "alive" in the customary sense. Robots, in addition, must be able to communicate with each other, being altruistic and sacrificing for the good of the communities of robot and man.

The unique and Hard Problem of robotic consciousness is the epistemological condition of consciousness. Science traditionally is the pulpit for public and non-personal observation. When the subjective aspects of observation are eliminated: *Susie is not warm; rather the measured temperature is 37°C,* a consensus is achieved. Reduction to the subjective domain, rather than the objective or third-person domain is part of the process. Its value is that it allows us to understand higher-level phenomena by relating them to lower-level phenomena. Neurologically-informed phenomenological reduction suggests that it may prove itself useful to consider conscious experience in terms of *protophenomena* or theoretical entities thought to be the constituents of phenomena, in this case, conscious thought.

In the most basic sense, protophenomena are similar to sense data, much like pixels, but more complex. Protophenomena also include expectations, moods, feelings, intentions, internal dialogs, imaginations and recollections. The unobservability of protophenomena questions the validity of their existence, comparing them to atoms in the 19th and early 20th centuries as theoretical entities. The possibility of a complex autonomous robot a similar subjective experience as a human cannot be answered without more knowledge of these activity sites in the brain.

"Robot the Robbie" may someday be as close—or closer—to you as Spot the dog or Fifi the cat. The robot of tomorrow may chat with you on line; and he may dance with you at the club. Whatever the case may be, it is most assuredly a promise that the robots of tomorrow will be deep thinkers.

23

CRITICAL THINKING, CREATIVE
THINKING AND GENIUS

The word "logic" comes from the Classical
Greek word *logos* (λόγος) which can be translated as
"sentence." In the New Testament it is translated as
"The Word"; and means: "God".[79] Other translations
of logos include "discourse," "reason," "ratio," and
"rule." *Critical thinking* is, even in its very earliest form,
considered as being informal logic. Both formal logic
and critical thinking are concerned with the principles
of correct reasoning. In this essay, I will concentrate
on some of the important aspects of critical thinking,
comparing it with its dysgenic or fraternal twin, *creative
thinking*.

Basically, critical thinking analyzes, evaluates and explains ideas, while creative thinking strives for an expansion of ideas without necessarily regarding their validity, soundness or appropriateness of content. When we compare critical thinking with creative thinking, we just might see the two realities as diametrically opposed. We must therefore use our own creative abilities to juxtapose these two systems of thought or "thought processes" in order to compare them. So, prepare yourself for a fantastic journey through your own realm of creative thought as you read through this essay.

Both critical thinking and creative thinking are enjoyable, productive and positive activities. And they are both emotive as well as rational, varying according to the contextual presentation and/or contents in which each moves or is "triggered." Whether it is a negative event that incites action or a positive catalyst makes little difference in regard to thoughtful activity and production. The critical thinker will be on the spot to analyze, synthesize, and postulate, explain and propose. Central to critical thinking is the identification and challenging of assumptions. The good critical thinker analyzes as he or she strives to identify the importance of context in an argument or any exposition of facts or assumptions, and, more often than not, "presumptions."[80] He then imagines alternatives and explores them. This intellectual practice of analysis, synthesis and creation leads to reflective skepticism, exposition, action, and the construction of intellectual concepts or concrete realities.

So, what *is* the definition of critical thinking? There has been a great deal of input from both philosophers and cognitive psychologists in the process of formulating a definition of critical thinking. There are many definitions "out there." Among them . . .

> [Critical thinking . . .] is the intellectually disciplined process of actively and skillfully conceptualizing, applying, synthesizing and/or evaluating experience reflecting, reasoning or communication as a guide to belief and action.[81]

In the opinion of the author of this essay, the best definitions are brief. So, in that light, I offer the following short definition for your perusal:

> Critical thinking is the disciplined activity of evaluating arguments or propositions and making judgments that can guide the development of beliefs and taking action.[82]

The above short, sweet and barely-compound sentence encompasses the subject matter completely and describes the march and compass of the process of critical thinking.

Critical thinking is a necessary tool of inquiry into one's personal life, and it is an essential liberating force in education. Critical thinking skills help us express the meaning and the significance of a wide variety of human experiences. In order to continue to live our lives well, we must confront our problems with courage, and we must analyze, evaluate, deduce, infer, and, finally, explain, stating the results of our reasoning with its justification in terms of evidence and the concepts ("The Problem") and the methods, the criteria, and the foundation or base from which the results of our critical thinking activities stem (a process or *Hegelian Dialectic*[83]). Lastly, we, as critical thinkers, present our reasoned explanation in the form of a cogent argument. Again, we deduce and infer relationships, examine statements and their validities and/or each one's credibility; and we come to conclusions. We critique and present rebuttals and form new arguments.

We are involved in the process and this is critical thinking in action. It is continuous. And it never stops. I daresay we are both creative and critical thinkers even when we dream . . . Fine-tuned critical thinking skills are unattainable without an in depth understanding of an argument and a broad knowledge base. We *all* have the wherewithal to explain our reasoning in a detailed, step-by-step (or point-by-point) manner. It is just a matter of finding the opportunity and taking action before we become paradigms of correct reasoning and creative thinking.

> *Critical thinking skills are an important attribute for success in the twenty-first century!*

Like critical thinking, creativity can be viewed as a process [within a system]. This process of thought within a scheme of systematic thinking is analogous to *The Language of Thought Hypothesis.*[84]

Creative individuals are highly intelligent. However, although creativity is inextricably tied to high intelligence, it is also something different from intelligence:

> Creativity is often defined as a parallel construct to intelligence, but it differs from intelligence in that it is not restricted to cognitive or intellectual reasoning or behavior. Instead, it is concerned with the complex mix of motives, conditions, personality factors, and even products.[85]

And, creativity is also different from innovation. Innovation is convergent thought, bringing familiar ideas back into people's experience, while creativity is essentially a divergent-thinking activity, at times expanding well beyond current thought and concepts.[86] Creativity can be thought of as an *aspect* of innovation since its goal is invention and exploration. But the goal of innovation is *transformation and implementation,* while creativity makes no such claims.

We can look at this aspect of innovation as being somewhat analogous to the corpus callosum in the brain which connects the two hemispheres: the right (creative, sentient) hemisphere "joins forces" with the left (logical, orderly) hemisphere. The union of the divergent with the convergent is the cooperative unity of the cerebral hemispheres resulting in *whole brain* output moving "under the same umbrella"—and the creation of something beautiful and/or useful or, perhaps—GIGO![87,88] A *bona fide* masterpiece may be born or another piece of drugstore junk may enter into and clutter our lives.

As we have seen, creative thinking is generally concerned with the creation or generation of ideas, processes, experiences and objects, or the explanation and expansion of these. The ideal critical thinker, for his part, analyzes, synthesizes, and then evaluates and suggests or explains.

> *Each thought process complements the other!*

The ideal critical thinker is insightful, inquisitive, knowledgeable, rational, unbiased, fair in evaluation; clear-thinking, honest, and a "good citizen." He offers us the results of his thinking (evaluation) in a "package" or presentation that is as precise as the queried and challenged subject and the circumstance permit. Good critical thinkers educate themselves and work toward this ideal. Critical thinkers are the foundation of rational and democratic societies. An ideal *creative thinker* is the *primum mobile* of societal change and advancement and, like his left-brained counterpart, is also a highly valued member of society. His or her somewhat risky—or very risky—ideas are the perfect complement to the staid and stable critical thinker's contributions. Both excellent critical thinkers and highly creative people tend to be whole-brained thinkers. The creative thinker is, undoubtedly, the "genius" of the pair—whether he be a poet, a novelist or a scientist.

Creative thinkers look at problems from various angles. They paint or express their thoughts for all of us to see and evaluate. They talk to us; and they produce many ideas, combining them and "mixing and matching." Many creative thinkers—and all creative geniuses—see relationships where the great majority sees none. Ideal creative thinkers manipulate thoughts that are the opposite of each other. They mold, write, manipulate, calculate, and paint them so they become useful concepts, ideas, theories and/or products and viable realities for us all.

Whether they begin as left-brain thinkers or right-brain thinkers, all creative geniuses are metaphorical and adventurous—and they have a tendency to be lucky!

24

PERSONALITY AND CREATIVITY

The creative act not only separates us from the apes it also provides us with a deep sense of being that reaches far beyond our view, leaving an outcome that adds to the richness and complex web of the future. It is therefore no wonder that creativity imparts great meaning in our lives. Our values, language, artistic expression, scientific understanding, literature, and technology are products of individual ingenuity that has since been transmitted to us through learning. Most of that which is important, interesting, and human is the result of someone's creativity. Only sex, sports, music, and religious ecstasy can compete with the creative act. And creativity remains central in our lives.

So what is it that creative individuals have that distinguishes them from the rest of us? First of all, they are very complex and show tendencies of thought and action that the majority of individuals sequester. Instead of being an "individual" each creative person is a myriad of thoughts and actions—a "creative multitude." Creative people also overflow with physical as well as mental energy. Do they have a genetic advantage? This abundance of internal energy appears to be generated and regenerated at will. So, instead of genetic superiority, their minds are highly focused and goal-oriented. They have the uncanny ability to turn their energy on and proceed like dynamos as they work and then they turn off their engines and take time to rest and "refuel."

Creative individuals are both sexual and celibate in their psychological makeup. Some express their libidos into sexuality, but continence tends to accompany superior achievement. They are intelligent yet naïve. Psychologists believe that creative individuals are endowed with high levels of general intelligence or "g."[89] Yet, beyond a certain IQ score (almost unanimously agreed upon as IQ 120) IQ does not necessarily imply higher creativity. Could it be true that a scientist with an IQ of 125 might be just as likely to win a Nobel Prize as his colleague who has an IQ of 180 . . . ? Perhaps, a case in point is Nobel Prize winning physicist, Richard Feynman, who *reputedly* had an IQ of 125. But could anyone seriously say that Feynman was *not* a genius? Was polymath Johann Wolfgang von Goethe (who *reputedly* had an IQ of 210) *more of a genius* than Richard Feynman?

The creative person is a well-above-average divergent[90] thinker. Divergent thinking demands fluency of thought as well as the ability to generate large quantities of novel ideas and to switch perspectives or ideas ("flexibility"). He or she possesses higher than average "levels" of originality in associative thinking. A tinge or shade of intellectual and emotional immaturity (or "childishness") may accompany deep insight. The creative individual is an extrovert and an introvert—proud yet humble; responsible and irresponsible; bold but timid. These characteristics on the surface appear oxymoronic; yet they coalesce nicely when they form part of the creative personality. Intrinsic motivation is usually a pronounced character trait of the creative individual. The ability to appreciate and admire his or her creation on its own merit is another important quality or "virtue" most creative people possess.

The most dreaded hour for many creative persons is when they sense that creativity is on the wane. They cannot work. Historical reality paints a more cheerful and hopeful scenario, however. Creativity can last well into the 80s and 90s—and beyond! Pablo Picasso and Grandma Moses are examples of creative accomplishment at its highest level in the very old.

When I am busy writing poetry (my favorite pastime) I often feel no need for sleep, food, or the necessity to communicate with others. In my state of self-induced "bliss," I "brainstorm" and write, creating metaphors and analogies in conjunction with the expression of my thoughts and feelings. I continue to write until I am satisfied with the end result. Then and only then I can sleep. The next day I usually rewrite the entire poem or story and compare it with last night's original. Sometime that evening or the next morning I edit my work and then submit it to one or two of my favorite magazines for publishing. More often than not, I keep my work "under wraps," waiting for that day when I can go public with it or store it indefinitely in the "deep freeze." If nothing else, I value the time and effort that went into the creation of my poem or story. Sometimes that is all I need, my own stamp of approval.

There are individuals who are endowed with all of the qualities of an artist, sculptor, poet, a short-story writer or novelist, etc., but they do not "behave" in a creative manner. Perhaps they choose not to be creative . . . ? Could it be that they just don't know they possess a creative "flair" . . . ? I believe there is a time and a place for everything and everyone. Almost instinctively, we *know* when we are ready to start and when we are ready to finish and move on.

Carpe diem!

25

THE RISE AND FALL OF
THE WORLD'S IQ

In a world where knowledge, ingenuity, creativity and opportunity are readily available, why is it that the world's IQ is declining? How could one conceive of the idea that IQ scores are declining? We have been led to believe otherwise. In this essay, I will attempt to give the reader a concise history of the Flynn Effect and current explanations of certain schools of thought.

Professor of moral philosophy and political science, James R. Flynn of the University of Otago in Dunedin, New Zealand studied IQ scores over time in the Twentieth Century and discovered that IQs worldwide appeared to be rising an amazing three points per decade—even more in some countries. Although several others had reached the same conclusion, Professor Flynn had worked hardest and longest in his attempts to analyze, exemplify, and explain this phenomenon. Hence, the eponymous Flynn Effect was born in 1986.

Now it appears that concepts of the Flynn Effect vis à vis one old and the most current hypotheses predict a steady decline in IQ scores throughout the world until the year 2050. In 1927, Lenz[91] hypothesized that intelligence across the world may have been in decline. He observed that intelligent couples were having fewer children than couples of average or lower intelligence. Psychologists Herrnstein and Murray[92] have confirmed this, showing that, in the United States, women with an IQ of 111 had 1.6 children while those with an average IQ of 81 had 2.6 children. This link between fewer children and the mothers' IQ scores is known as "dysgenic fertility." Lynn and Harvey calculated this global, genotypic decline in IQ comparing the world's average IQ scores for two successive generations, 1950 and 2000. The IQ scores came out to be 92.75 in 1950 and 90.31 in 2000. Hardly a significant difference; yet, it appeared as a predictor for future generations. For the next 50 years the decline will be high. It has been predicted that genotypic IQ test scores will decline more than they have in previous generations because fertility rates for high-IQ individuals are expected to be lower in the two generations between 2000 and 2050.

If genotypic[93] IQs are headed for a fall, it also appears that the positive effects from the Flynn Effect are becoming scarcer and they may be subject to the law of diminishing returns. As a matter of fact, the Flynn Effect has ceased to be in certain developed or so-called "First World" nations. For example, a study of 11-12 year olds in Great Britain showed a decline of 4.3 IQ points in a decade. As the Flynn Effect gradually goes into hibernation, it can be inferred that *both* genotypic and phenotypic[94] intelligence will eventually undergo a global decline. As regards the hypotheses that the Flynn Effect is still "going strong" Robert Lindsay[95] observes:

> One argument is that the Flynn Effect is not a real intelligence rise at all, since it is not *on* real intelligence. "The FE gains are not gains in intelligence at all, they are zero, nothing, null." He goes on to say "This is not correct, but the argument is interesting. First we need to understand what the FE is and what it means. Then we need to what *g i*s and what it means. [. . .] There has been indeed an FE rise on g, but only on one component of g". Further, the post criticizes the whole notion of seeing intelligence purely through the lens of *g* as senseless and meaningless, not to mention flat out wrong.[96]

Alan Griswold believes:

> [. . .] if the impressive Flynn effect statistics from the Twentieth Century are

telling us anything at all, it is from sheer momentum alone that the Flynn effect can be expected to remain with us, and sustain us, for a considerable time to come [. . .] If the Flynn effect has ended, then so has the course of human progress. To embrace such an absurdity would be to misperceive what the Flynn effect has been trying to tell us, it would be to misconceive Professor Flynn's question "What is intelligence."[97]

It seems to me that Alan Griswold has "placed all of his eggs in one basket." He seems to be wagering that the Flynn Effect will continue as it has well into the Twenty-First Century and beyond as a sort of perennial savior of intelligence for the survival of the human race and a standard bearer for progress. He relies on notions of a spaciotemporal nature. He envisions a world progressively more spacial, more temporal, and coalescing with a very highly patterned environment. Griswold is convinced, and he proselytizes that the end of the Flynn Effect will mark the end of the human race: "It is not the Flynn effect that should be frightening us, but rather its end."[98]

In many areas phenotypic intelligence has been increasing (the Flynn Effect) while genotypic intelligence is decreasing due to the negative association between intelligence and that which is known as "dysgenic fertility." Gains of as much as 7.5 IQ points in phenotypic intelligence are much greater than the 0.43 IQ points per generation in the world-wide genotypic IQ that had been estimated for the period 1950-2000.

The situation in the industrially developed world appears to follow the lead of the United States and a handful of other developed nations in so far as the phenotypic IQ has been increasing at a greater rate as a result of environmental improvements.[99] In Norway, Sweden, Denmark, Great Britain and Australia, phenotypic intelligence has stabilized and now is declining. In spite of this, former "Third World" developing nations have shown an *increase* (the Flynn Effect at its best) and this will reduce the phenotypic intelligence gap between economically developed nations and those that are on the path to industrial and economic development. Kenya and the small Caribbean island nation of Dominica are prime examples of the latter. When we all are at a par, environmental improvements in the economically blessed nations will cease. The continuance of dysgenic fertility will trigger a global decline in both genotypic and phenotypic intelligence. The obvious and most logical solution may be some form of eugenics, reversing dysgenic fertility. Perhaps not so obvious is the controversy and philosophical/ theological/scientific brouhaha that will most certainly ensue at the mere mention of the word "eugenics." What must be avoided at all costs is authoritarianism, i.e., similar to the Chinese model: one child per family rule adopted in the early 1980s. Following the lead of the controversial, "licenses for parenthood" would only be granted to couples with a certain level of intelligence.

In conclusion, in order to nip dysgenic fertility in the bud and the ensuing decline of genotypic IQ, eugenics demands that embryos be scanned and selected and then pass a sort of "prenatal IQ test." These embryos must also posses other desirable qualities.

26

THE OPTIMIST'S ADVANTAGE

Don't classify people and situations in advance,
wait until you know what's in front of you.
> ~ Richard Wiseman[100]

A person's outlook, or Weltanschauung,[101] has more to do with his or her happiness than whatever else might happen to that person. A positive outlook, an intelligent and healthy optimism, is a wise philosophy in both difficult times and during good times. We experience high points and low points in the vicissitudes of life, how we resolve our problems determines who we are.

Are you an intelligent optimist, a pessimist, or somewhere in between? Both the intelligent optimist and the pessimist are realists in their own particular way. Let us look closer at these personality types, especially optimism, and determine where we recognize ourselves.

Briefly, optimism is a doctrine that says the world is the best possible world. The intelligent optimist has the inclination to put the most favorable face and structure upon actions and events, anticipating the best outcome. The other side of the coin is pessimism, which is defined by Miriam Webster[102] as 1) An inclination to emphasize adverse aspects, conditions, and possibilities, or to expect the worst possible outcome; 2) a. The doctrine that reality is essentially evil; b. The doctrine that evil will overbalance happiness in life.

When we observe those around us, we easily note the difference between the intelligent optimist and the pessimist. The intelligent optimist tends to find the positive side of the problem while the pessimist makes no such effort. The pessimist always sees the glass half-empty, to use a tired, but useful, cliché. Throwing his hands up in frustration or exasperation with a "That's it!" "I can't do it!" "It's over!" The prototypical pessimist is the original "I can't" person or "naysayer." On the other hand, the intelligent optimist makes a considered conscious choice, as opposed to an impulsive choice. The intelligent optimist is like the inventor: He or she won't quit.

Listen to your thoughts, take heed and make the changes you deem necessary to become a more positive, a happier and a more successful human being, whatever your definition of success may be. If your thinking tends to swing more to the "negative" side of the pendulum, balance may be what you need. *Excessive negative thinking is unrealistic and harmful.* Analyze the meaning of that negative thought that may be eating away at your brain, extricate the ulcer of a problem, or, if you cannot, do your best to put it behind you. All great men and women learn from experience—both their positive and negative experiences.

Much negative thinking is rooted in past experiences. It may work for an abused child who expects the worst from people and events. He or she never gets good things anyway, so why should he expect them? The end result is always the same; and he learned at a very early age that he will never be disappointed or hurt. However, as adults we are obligated by maturity and the mores of our respective societies to take responsibility into our own hands. How can we let negativity or extreme pessimism destroy our future . . . ? Meeting this challenge with empty, unreal, hopeless and helpless thoughts will do us no good whatsoever. When we catch our negativity, let it simultaneously drop from our hands; let us analyze and determine its true meaning and challenge; and, let us move on with a realistic plan and an "upbeat attitude."

There are many benefits to being an intelligent optimist. To name just a few, the intelligent optimist is generally happier than his pessimistic counterpart; he usually lives longer than the negative thinker; he is a positive thinker; and, the intelligent optimist usually achieves his goals because he never gives up or drowns himself in cauldron self-pity. The intelligent optimist may even achieve his goals faster than the meticulously-negative-thinking pessimist. And, just as a pessimist can be boring or even annoying to be around, an intelligent optimist can make us feel more energetic and positive. The pessimist is obsessed with the problem, while the intelligent optimist focuses on the solution. He rebounds from failure and other defeats in life's challenges faster than the pessimist, who may view failure as inevitable. The pessimist does not move forward in order to help himself. In order to reverse the pessimist's perceived "helpless" situation, afflatus of the intelligently-optimistic kind is necessary to take advantage of the opportunity and seize the day,[103] transforming something ugly or cheap into something beautiful or valuable, and being creative. One of the primary advantages the intelligent optimist has over the pessimist is his lateral thinking.

"Optimist" is not synonymous with "Pollyanna."[104] There are academics and psychology researchers who disagree with the *rose-colored glasses* approach to living and resolving our day-to-day problems. Professor Joseph Forgas believes "Negative moods trigger more attentive, careful thinking to the external world."[105,106] However, negativity can cause one to commit errors, perhaps worsening the pessimist's state of mind. (I wonder how many paranoid optimists there are . . .?)

We cope emotionally, trying to make ourselves feel better using strategies such as "looking at the bright side" (*emotion-focused coping*); or, if we use *problem-focused coping*; we try to change the course of events in order to get to the root of our problem or stressful situation. Each of us must analyze, decide, plan, and take appropriate action to resolve the issue. The type of situation will usually dictate which is the correct method. So we must obviously be flexible. There are rules of thumb to guide us: emotion-focused coping is more appropriate for situations when it is too late to remedy or change the situation. Emotion-focused coping can have disastrous effects when our actions determine the consequences. We must be careful with our emotions and not let them rule our thoughts and dictate our behavior. Problem-focused coping, then, is the most effective way to deal with stress and problems when our efforts really make the difference. Yet, problem-focused coping can be thought of as a sort of "perfectionism" that may cause "unrealistic expectations." We cannot change the unchangeable.

Optimism and pessimism are two different philosophies and strategies for coping with an overly-complex and unpredictable world:

> [. . .] both optimism and pessimism have important roles to play in people's lives. Being optimistic allows people to pursue their goals in a positive way: they dream a bigger and better dream, which they can work their way towards. On the other hand, being pessimistic may help people reduce their natural anxieties and to perform better. Also, pessimists like to hear what the problems were so they can correct them. Again, part of why pessimists

generate these negative thoughts is that it helps them perform better.[107]

We have seen that optimism, in general, appears to be a more suitable state of mind and philosophy than pessimism for the human condition, if only because optimists are happier than their pessimistic brothers and sisters. Serendipity tends to smile upon those of us with a more relaxed attitude and approach to life. The optimist must be a realist, but not a negativist. On the other hand he or she should also avoid being a "Pollyanna." And, for those pessimists among us— for the life of you, don't be "Chicken Little"![108]

27

THE *G*-FACTOR

Whether we like it or not, we are all born with different characteristics, abilities and potentials. Some of us are taller, better-looking, darker, lighter, more creative or with more athletic ability than others among us. Most notably, and sometimes most painfully, we are born unequal in intellectual potential: an unavoidable, irreparable fact of life.

Psychologist Charles Spearman postulated the Two-Factor Theory of intelligence in 1927 as a theory of trait organization based on the statistical analysis of IQ test scores. Spearman advanced the theory that all intellectual factors have a single factor which is called the *g* factor[109] as well as a number of specific or "s" factors. These specific factors refer to separate, single and specific activities and abilities. He explored the statistical interrelations of scores on various tests and concluded that a positive correlation between any two mental functions must be attributed to the *g*-factor, since "s" factors have low correlations among them. Spearman reasoned that since the *g*-factor runs through all mental abilities and predicts an individual's performance, it would be of no use to measure specific ("s") factors, since each one operates in only a single activity. Spearman proposed that the *g*-factor is a sort of "mirror" or reflection of one's intelligence;[110] and he hypothesized that *g*, "general intelligence," was the primary reason for positive relations among the various scores on IQ tests. In a group of IQ tests, the test that measures most accurately *g* is the test that has the highest correlations with all the others.

"*g*-loading" is the correlation between a test and *g* in which the score reflects general mental ability. Most *g*-loaded tests have at least one form of abstract reasoning. A common, but still unproven view is that, perhaps, *g* is the genetically-determined essence of intelligence.

The accepted best measure of *g* is Raven's Progressive Matrices, a test of visual reasoning. The RPM is controversial because there are substantial gender differences on the test that are not found when computed from any array of other tests. The Raven Progressive Matrices is a "culture fair" IQ test; and, it is, therefore, one of the best "*g*-loaded" tests.[111]

Other indicators of general intelligence are Elementary Cognitive Tasks. ECTs are simple tasks that apparently require little intelligence but correlate strongly with full scale IQ tasks. The pressing of two buttons in response to the options in a task while a third button is pressed and held down from the beginning of the test may or may not obtain a right answer. When the tested individual chooses the correct answer, he removes his hand from the start button. Reaction time is usually measured in fractions of a second. Reaction time correlates strongly with g, while movement time correlates less strongly. ECTs are a parallel link between classical IQ testing and biological structures such as MRIs.[112]

Spearman's Law of Diminishing Returns, or, the "ability differentiation hypothesis," states that positive correlations among different cognitive abilities are weaker among more intelligent sub-groups of individuals. That is, the SLDR predicts that the g-factor will account for a smaller proportion of individual score differences in cognitive score differences in cognitive tests at high scores on the g-factor. The SLDR is most effectively applied to representative samples of individuals rather than randomly. A common factor model, allowing the relation between the factor and its indicators, should be non-linear in nature. A 2009 study by Trucker-Drob found that a general factor accounted for approximately 75 percent of the variation in seven cognitive abilities among very low IQ adults.[113] In contrast, a g-factor accounted for approximately 30 percent of the variation in the abilities of very high IQ adults.

The overall *g*-load of a test correlates with heritability. The sometimes "notorious" psychologist Arthur Jensen agrees with and supports a "genetic *g*"; and he does not believe that it (the *g*-factor) is merely a statistical device. The degree of heritability can be estimated; and methods of doing this include comparing siblings' intelligence scores on an array of IQ tests, and the degree of inbred depression from cousin marriages, etc. The strongest biological correlates for *g* include mass of the prefrontal lobe; overall brain mass; cortical thickness; and the rate of glucose metabolization within the brain. *G* also correlates with overall body size, albeit less strongly. Current research suggests that the heritability of *g* is approximately 0.85, which is even higher than that for IQ itself. It appears, therefore, that the heritability of most test performances must be attributable to *g*.[114,115]

G and brain size highly correlate. MRI[116] studies on twins have shown that frontal gray matter volume is significantly correlated with *g* and heritability. The correlation between brain size and *g* is linked to multiple genetic and mental disorders. Schizophrenia can effect one's score on an intelligence test, after accounting for complications such as socioeconomic factors or status. The average person suffering from schizophrenia will score as much as one standard deviation lower — 15 points on the Wechsler scale — on an IQ test than a person not affected with that disease. And many other chromosomal abnormalities affect *g* and result in decreased intellectual abilities.[117]

The lofty content of many IQ tests and their positive implications in educational success can give the impression that *g* is only a measure of academic ability. But *g* also predicts job performance. The more complex the job, the better the *g*-factor predicts job performance. In fact, general intelligence predicts job performance better than any other trait. The value of mental tests and their measurement of *g* rise with the complexity and higher status of the job. As a task increases in complexity, the higher the *g* levels become; lower *g* levels then become even more of a handicap. These high levels of g and low levels of g are our reflections in the success or failure of our daily activities and our relationships.

> People somewhat below average are 88 times more likely to drop out of high school, seven times more likely to be jailed, and five times more likely as adults to live in poverty than people with a somewhat-above average IQ. Below-average individuals are 50 percent more likely to be divorced than those in the above-average category.[118]

Many psychologists have challenged the validity of the *g*-factor in general intelligence tests, most notably psychologist Howard Gardner and anthropologist Stephen Jay Gould. Gardner's *Theory of Multiple Intelligences*[119] places general intelligence in the hands of a series of specific abilities, some of which we excel in, and others where we are weaker or less intelligent. Most psychologists and psychometricians believe that intelligence is akin to many other scientific concepts, and intelligence tests, like scientific theories, are correctly measured by testing and retesting.

Our IQ usually varies over time depending upon any one or more of a multitude of factors: how we feel on the day we sit for the test; our age (some people attain their best scores in childhood, while others do better as they age and mature); and, naturally, our attitude towards the proctor or the test itself. If you are determined to give multiple answers instead of the best response to the question; and answer straightforward questions in a divergent or "out of the box" fashion, I can almost guarantee you will not score as high as you are capable. I'm thinking of the series of tests: the WAIS IQ tests (Wechsler Adult Intelligence Scale) designed by David Wechsler. The WAIS, by its very design, demands total interaction and a good rapport between the psychometrician and the individual tested. Despite its seeming rigorous demands, the WAIS can be an enjoyable one and one-half to three hours spent in a psychologist's office. And, depending upon where you take the WAIS, it may be either quite expensive or a real bargain.

28

INTELLIGENT INTUITION

The heart has its reasons, which reason cannot know.

~Blaise Pascal

In order to avoid confusion at the outset, let us f irst distinguish between "instinct" and "intuition." Briefly, instinct is a genetically programmed behavior that the human species share with animals. Instinctual behavior is not the result of learning, and it can be seen across all members of a species. "Intuition," as defined by the Oxford English Dictionary, "is the ability to acquire knowledge without inference or the use of reason." Undoubtedly, there are many ways to define intuition, but some are problematic. The conscious act of reflecting on intuition is precisely what intuition is *not*. In a nutshell, intuition is your brain on autopilot processing information out of the conscious awareness that it is operating. In other words, intuition is non-conscious thinking.

How then does intuition work? When we think in images and we feel, we are experiencing a function of the subconscious mind which is called "intuition." "Sensual thinking,"[120] as intuition is commonly called, is the expression of images, visions, feelings, etc. brought to life and sometimes to creative artistic expression. As poet Stephen Spender called it, "the logic of images" It is not words we are looking for, rather sensual associations or feelings.

Sensual thinking is "common sense thinking," not only for poets but for all of us. Composer George Antheil strove to write his music following his "inner pattern," his inner logic. The practice resulted in musical form. And mathematician Norbert Weiner discovered that his bodily feelings, his sensual thinking, could act as temporary symbols for a mathematical situation. No matter how private or how intimate the memory, an imaginative articulation of images and feelings follows. This sensation, "meta-logic" or "super-logic," has its own rules. Conceptually, meta-logic is very close to intuition—if not intuition itself. Words rarely accompany intuitive insight—we "see"; we "get the picture"; we "feel"; and, we "just know."

Women tend to excel in nonverbal sensitivity. For example, research suggests they surpass men in discerning whether a male-female couple is genuinely romantic or a posed pair of phonies. Some men are more empathetic than the average woman, but the intuition-gender gap appears real, for some reason. More than men, women base knowledge on intuitive and personal grounds, and they tend to be more subjective in their preferences and decision making.

During our subconscious intuitive state, our brains process information apart from our awareness that it is happening. We rely on intuition for rote tasks, but what about more complex situations? Business people and stock market buyers and traders commonly make "gut level" decisions during the process of high-stakes decision making. All of us make sound judgments about food and relationships using our "non-conscious" processes. However, conscious, reflective thinking often sabotages our preferences; hence, we make the wrong decision. Intuition is a big part of decision-making, but the negative side is that intuition often errs. People sometimes fool themselves, and even the most intelligent people make predictable and costly errors. People from all walks of life and all social strata can fall into illusory intuitions. "Studies suggest, for instance, that people mis-predict the durability and intensity of their emotions after a romantic breakup, losing an election, winning a game and being insulted."[121]

Because intuitive thinking is non-linguistic, it may be very difficult to express one's thoughts to others. Perhaps "mind melding" and machines capable of transmitting inner experience will be common someday. For the time being, however, intuition is a reliable way of knowing, and it is valuable in many circumstances. And we should not fear not knowing every reason why we feel the way we do. Our decision or preference is many times correct without further analysis or consideration. Although there is no substitute for analytical thinking and gathering information about any task or situation we confront, there are times we may comfortably let our brains slide into "cruise control."

In conclusion, intuition feeds our professional and personal expertise, our creativity, our love and our spiritually. We think smarter knowing we have learned from our erroneous decisions, whether they we reasoned decisions or intuitive.

29

INTELLIGENCE, GENETICS AND ENVIRONMENT

English scientist Francis Galton (1822-1911), a cousin of Charles Darwin, started the debate and controversy over heredity and the environment, better known as the "nature versus nurture debate," more than a century ago. In 1865, primarily due to reading a book written by Darwin called *Origin of Species,* Galton began to study heredity. Galton then concentrated his efforts on studying human intelligence and its variations. He was a fervent believer in heredity and that personal success was due to qualities that were passed down from parents to offspring through heredity. In his lifetime Galton made significant contributions to genetics and psychology, among other disciplines. He was a proponent of "nature" in the "nature versus nurture debate," supporting the role of heredity. He eventually introduced the method of twin studies to help determine the different contributions of nature and nurture.[122] His monumental work in psychology is entitled *English Men of Science: Their Nature and Nurture.*

Is intelligence a product of heredity or is it a product of the environment? Human intelligence can be thought of as a very special ability that allows us to think abstractly, analyze, reason, plan and resolve problems using our experience as we progress through life. Thus, intelligence is not *only* a special ability to solve problems on an I.Q. test, rather it is primarily the ability to interpret and understand the unique and complex environment in which we live. Our intelligence tells us what we should do and what we should not do according to the dictates of our conscience and our moral codes, societal values (mores) and our wisdom.

Given the above attributes at our disposal, we may ask ourselves: "Where does it all come from?" There are those who believe that genetics (nature) accounts for 80 percent to 100 percent of our overall intelligence, while others claim that genetics and environment (nurture) are equal (or "almost equal") partners in the ultimate determination of our mental abilities.

"While genes have an impact on our behavior, the environment is still responsible for the behavioral variability between us."[123] Does the previous sentence ring true or is it a politically correct compromise of scientific fact? Let's look at the facts: First of all, genes encapsulate our evolutionary experience. Therefore, genetic-environmental interaction can be understood as our past environmental interactions with our present environmental interactions. That is, we are hard-wired (genetically) to interact with our environment. Secondly, in the process of our development, our genes assume the presence of our environment. That is, we adapt ourselves (our genes) to our environment. As a consequence, human behavior only responds to things for which we were designed, much as an elevator responds with a movement up or down when an appropriate button is pushed. An elevator does not (usually) respond to a human voice command to go up or down (unless it was designed and programmed to do so). The debate over whether intelligence is mostly hereditary or environmental has raged on fiercely for going on two centuries. The nature versus nurture debate has remained without a clear conclusion. Both camps have presented thoroughly convincing arguments and hypotheses.

Nature versus nurture—Who is right? An understanding of the human genome makes it clear that *both* sides in the debate are partly right, since nature (heredity, genetics) gives us our inborn abilities and traits while nurture (the environment) takes our genetically given abilities and shapes them as we learn and mature.[124] But a 50/50 compromise is not the end of the debate. Now, scientists scrap over how much human intelligence and other abilities are determined by genetics and how much by the environment. Behaviorists[125] believe that, while genetic tendencies exist, genetics does not matter and our behavioral aspects originate only from environmental factors of our upbringing; hence, intelligence is environmental (nurtured). Harvard psychologist B.F. Skinner's[126] early experiments that produced pigeons that could dance, do figure eights and play tennis contributed to his fame as a proponent of environmentalism in the nature versus nurture intelligence debate. The nurture camp might ask:

Is the way we behave engraved in us before we are born, or has it developed over time in response to our experience?" The nature camp responds: "Of course our responses to stimuli have been engraved in us while we were still in utero. And of course our behaviors have developed over time in response to experiences. That is, we have been hard-wired in our ancestral genes to respond a certain way to environmental stimuli and to react and adjust our behaviors according to the demands of our present environment. Our genes encapsulate experiences from our evolutionary past. Thus genes interacting with the environment must be considered as past environment interacting with present environment. Our genes are designed in such a way as to anticipate or predict certain environmental factors; therefore, variability in behavioral outcome may be 100 percent explained by the scenario manifest in our design (i.e. our genes).

Human behavior is the result of thousands of genes interacting with each other and the environment. Here is a simple example of an argument in the nature versus nurture debate as it refers to "genius":

> The key factor separating genius from merely accomplished is not divine spark. It's not I.Q. Instead, it's deliberate practice [. . .] Public discussion is smitten by genetics and what we're hard-wired to do. And it's true that genes place a leash on our capacities. But the brain is also phenomenally plastic. We construct ourselves through behavior.[127]

The information in the above quote is quite misleading. According to David Brooks, you can take anyone off the street and turn them into a genius. All that is necessary is that they have a sense of affinity, a desperate need for success and the drive to sustain them ("ambition"). Brooks ignores the fact that our interests are innate, coming from our genes. They are triggered genetically, and then they adapt to the environment.

We all differ genetically. We have different desires, cravings and passions. Motivation and drive are innate (genetic). They are not qualities that can be infused. And they are *rare* qualities. Perhaps this is why the genius is either highly praised or painfully ignored during his or her lifetime.

Genes account for our motivation, personality, intelligence, ambition, criminality[128] and leadership skills; and these traits and abilities are all part of our genetic makeup, and not in our nurture. Nature endows us with these inborn abilities and traits; nurture takes these genetic inheritances and molds them as we learn and mature. If genetics did not play the major role in the formation of our abilities and traits, then fraternal twins, reared under the same conditions, would be alike, regardless of differences in their genes. While studies have shown they do more closely resemble each other than non-twin siblings, they also show these same salient similarities when reared apart, as in similar studies with monozygotic ("identical") twins.

In August of 2011, *Science Daily* published news of the first direct link to human intelligence. This was the first study[129] to find a genetic contribution in testing people's DNA for genetic variations. The team of scientists studied two types of intelligence in more than 3500 people in the north of England and Scotland. The results indicate that 40 percent to 50 percent of the differences could be traced to genetic differences. The author of the researching team's paper, Doctor Neil Pendleton of the Center for Integrated Genetic Research in Manchester, England reported:

> This is the first reported research to examine intelligence of healthy, older adults using a comprehensive survey; we were able to show a substantial genetic contribution to our ability to think.[130] We can now use the findings to better understand how these genes interact with each other and the environment . . . With our collaborators; we will take this work

forward to find biological mechanisms that could maintain our intellectual abilities and well being in late life.[131]

The study confirms the previous findings of the twins' research; but that research could not identify which genes were and were not contributing to our cognitive ability.[132]

> "As reported in a forthcoming article in the journal *Psychological Science*, they found that in nearly every case, the hypothesized genetic pathways failed to replicate. In other words, intelligence could not be linked to specific genes that were tested."[133]

So, who is right—nature or nurture? Should we sit on the fence undecided, like "mug-wumps,"[134] or should we be really risky and take sides in the debate? Perhaps the intelligent, well-balanced ("open-minded") way to score the centuries-old nature versus nurture debate just may be to call it a draw . . . ?

In conclusion: an observation: Identification of intelligence-specific genes may be a long way off. The problem appears to be one of strategy and technology: how to conduct research and with what tools. Modern science does not yet have the proper tools to perform the much-needed research.

30

MULTIPLE INTELLIGENCES

In the early 1980s, psychology professor Howard Gardner opened the window to multiple intelligences, claiming his theory casts more light on the fact that humans exist together in a multitude of contexts and that these contexts exercise and nourish our different intelligences. Gardner's *Theory of Multiple Intelligences* is opposed to the traditional "psychometric view" of intelligence inasmuch as it does not espouse the *g*-factor per se rather the idea that human intelligence manifests itself automatically in seven predominant intelligences. These intelligences are *linguistic; musical; logical-mathematical; spatial bodily-kinesthetic; interpersonal; intrapersonal;* and, *natural.* Each of these is manifested in culturally "intelligent" behaviors with normal adults' different profiles of strengths and weaknesses across the spectrum of these intelligences.

As a consequence of Howard Gardner's Multiple Intelligence model, there was a significant impact on education with schools developing broader and more responsive approaches to assessment and a more diverse curriculum to help in the individual intelligences of each student. Some primary schools and secondary schools (high schools) became SUMIT schools (Schools Using Multiple Intelligences Theory).

Gardner claimed there was no *g*—or general— factor of intelligence, and he also provided *no* theoretical specification of what his proposed intelligences constitute nor how they function at social, cognitive or logical levels. Hence, an ideal accumulation of evidence for the theory of multiple intelligences became problematic. So, although challenging and appealing, there is no evidence for autonomous intelligences of the Howard Gardner type—rather just the opposite! It has been shown that diverse abilities are generally correlated and pay tribute to an "executive function." But there *is* more to intelligence than just *g*.[135] Currently, the number of quantifiable intelligences extends beyond Gardner's original Theory of Multiple Intelligences.

A notable example of theories of multiple intelligences is Robert Sternberg's *Triarchic Theory of Intelligence*, which also downplays the concept of a *g*-factor.[136] Sternberg suggests three principal or dominant intelligences: analytical intelligence (which is componential and approximates the original notion of *g* and is the type of intelligence measured by IQ tests); creative intelligence (which is experiential and involves insight, synthesis and the ability to creatively respond to novel structures); and practical intelligence (which is contextual and involves the ability to solve real-life problems, that is, "common sense"). Sternberg's Triarchic Theory of Intelligence attempts to explain how each of these predominant intelligences contributes to our "mental self-management" (executive functioning) via (a) performance components; (b) knowledge acquisition components; and, (c) metacomponents. At the base of this hierarchy are the elemental performance components, the information-processing mechanisms involved in the execution of sequential operations such as encoding, inference and response selection. Knowledge acquisition components are those processes that store information and include memory. These components, in turn, will evolve or create performance components in the service of their own functions. At the top of Sternberg's processing hierarchy are metacomponents. These "executive processes" are responsible for planning task solutions and monitoring feedback from the performance and knowledge acquisition components. According to Sternberg, the major individual differences related to intelligence are found in the metacomponents processes. In other words, the domain of "intelligence" involves the problem-solving strategies (higher-level components) rather than the information-processing (low-level components) that implement the problem-solving routines.

Sternberg's Triarchic Theory of Intelligence is more like a statement or description of how intelligence is manifested, rather than an explanation of the process. Creative and practical intelligences should not be *equal* in importance to analytical intelligence; rather they both should be *subservient* to it. In its current state, Gardner's Theory of Multiple Intelligences may be no more than a list of talents characteristic to humankind. The "theory" can lead to confusion and errors in application.

IN CONCLUSION . . .

In *Concepts of Intelligence* we start out with a discussion about polyglottism. We learn that it is the ability to speak at least three languages in addition to one's own native tongue. We meet several hyper-polyglots, or people with the ability to speak a dozen languages or more. Among them are Pope John Paul II, American baseball star, civil rights activist and actor Paul Robeson and 19th century Italian Cardinal Giuseppe Mezzofanti. As we progress we also learn that there are certain similarities between so-called "mad men," or those afflicted with mental illness, and a group that is not so harshly disparaged, highly creative individuals. The common factors between these two groups are a certain degree of intelligence, interest in creative projects, fantasy proneness, creative ability and low levels of latent inhibition. Poetry and the plastic arts is the common junction for a good number of these highly creative types. Some individuals afflicted with mental illness as well as their highly creative counterparts may each possess the DARPP-32 gene, a brain circuitry optimizer. Poets Sylvia Plath and Edgar Allan Poe; Impressionist painter Vincent Van Gogh and former British Prime Minister Winston Churchill all suffered from some form of bipolar disorder (also known as manic-depressive illness). Nobel Prize-winning economist and mathematician John Forbes Nash and Beat Generation poet Jack Kerouac are in the paranoid schizophrenic diagnostic. As we read on, we learn that the Theory of Multiple Intelligences was proposed by psychologist Howard Gardner, a disbeliever in the concept of IQ and "general intelligence" (or "*g*"). Gardner's proposed seven intelligences in his Theory of Multiple Intelligences stand in diametrical opposition to the majority of hypotheses and theories that deal with the concepts of IQ and "*g*" and the measure (or "mismeasure") of intelligence. There are, of course, theories that can be compared and contrasted with one another other using the same concepts and the same lexicon, but there are others that cannot be so easily evaluated for their respective merits and similarities. Howard Gardner's Theory of Multiple Intelligences and Robert Sternberg's Triarchic Theory of Intelligence are two such examples. Sternberg's Triarchic Theory of Intelligence is more like a statement or description of how intelligence is manifested rather than an explanation of the process.

While writing the essays that would eventually be incorporated into Concepts of Intelligence, I faced the problem of logical continuity. How should I follow "The Mozart Effect"? For that matter, how did I precede it . . . ? The latter thought put me correctly in context. I decided I would proceed in the most functional and convenient way possible. I hope I did not confuse or annoy you in the process. There is no intended "logical progression" from one essay to the next in Concepts of Intelligence because there is just no logical need for it. Instead, I have logically—or otherwise—presented you with a virtual motley crew of seemingly independent concepts. But these concepts rely heavily upon one another in helping you understand the terminology and explanations defined and discussed herein.

As the author, my challenge in Concepts of Intelligence is to keep you informed of the variegated ideas and manifestations of intelligence (concepts and theories— both old and new) and help you stay interested in—and stay focused on— the investigation of that mysterious entity we call "intelligence." Concepts of Intelligence offers you several working definitions of intelligence, and they all share common elements.

I cover a "limited spectrum" (excuse the oxymoron) in Concepts of Intelligence, yet I may fall a bit short. But not really! Concepts of Intelligence is meant to be a primer, not a primary textbook. And, there are historical theories and concepts I do not discuss, and I generally leave the future in the most capable hands of, well—the future!

Whether we are primarily left-brain people or right-brain people, each of us tend to be "cerebrally ambidextrous," relying on the corpus callosum to relay information from right hemisphere to left hemisphere and from left to right, while sharing our observations, insights and creative impulses ("afflatus") as our cerebral faculties work in unison." So, I wonder, does the manifestation of "creativity" equal the manifestation of "genius" . . . ? All of the great geniuses in the history of the world are commonly referred to as "creative geniuses," so it appears the two concepts may, in fact, be (relatively) synonymous. Creativity is—at the very least—the kindling of genius. And there is much that can be said about genius, genius potential and genius actualization, but this will have to wait a short time until a sequel to Concepts of Intelligence is published or, perhaps, you have done own skilled research. Concepts of Intelligence has as many essays about creativity: "Does Our Creativity Decline as We Grow Older?"; Critical Thinking, Creative Thinking And Genius; "Creativity and Personality"; etc. as there are essays that primarily deal with our general intelligence: "The G Factor"; "Are We Smarter than Our Ancestors?—the Flynn Effect"; "The Mozart Effect"; etc. The simple fact of the matter is that we must use our IQs (or "intelligence") creatively and in a productive manner.

Concepts of Intelligence defines and examines various personality types: the optimist, the pessimist, the introvert, the extrovert and, yes, the ambivert. Concepts of Intelligence also examines computers and artificial intelligence (A. I.) at some length. The concepts of WI-FI and building your own home or office or local area network (LAN) as well as computer robotics each merit essays. Nevertheless, there are a number of elements I touch upon only lightly or do not cover at all. I leave these latter concepts to you—to your imagination and your spirit of adventure.

I include the essay on animal intelligence not only to satisfy the animal lovers in our midst but also to satiate my own curiosity. I happen to be the primary source of food and lodging for five very smart cats and one absolute genius of a black Labrador Retriever. So, it seems we are all animal lovers to one extent or another. And we are, in fact, animals ourselves albeit "only human."

Within Concepts of Intelligence there is a very appealing essay: "Are Beautiful People More Intelligent?" This essay apparently touched a raw nerve of a good number of Mensans in the online LinkedIn Mensa International forum after it was published in the Mensa International Journal. The essay was both very popular and very controversial in that forum. My conclusion states that the Kanzawa-Kovar Theorem ("beautiful people are more intelligent") is suspect since there is little evidence to support it. It would appear then that Albert Einstein is not the homely genius or the exception that proves the Kanazawa-Kovar rule rather he is an important cog in the dynamic wheel of universal brilliance. Further research is necessary in order to determine if "beautiful people" in fact tend to be smarter (or dumber than) the rest of us. Do genes for beauty ("beautiful genes") pair with genes for brains, the elusive intelligent gene(s) . . . ? This is interesting in an aesthetic sense but really unimportant in any useful or practical sense.

I discuss certain aspects of genetics in the second essay of Concepts of Intelligence, entitled "Birth Order and Intelligence." The concept of the intelligence gene is given "extended coverage" in Chapter 29: "Intelligence, Genetics and Environment." The nature versus nurture (genetics versus environment) debate continues and the elusive intelligence gene remains at large. Undoubtedly it exists, yet there may be hundreds—perhaps even thousands—of genes that contribute to our cognitive function. New scientific tools and research methods must first be developed in order to continue with an effective investigation to locate; study, and label the human intelligence gene(s). This very worthy project should be "next" on the list of important tasks for the scientific community.

"Phrenology: Protoscience/Pseudoscience"; "Moctezuma's Revenge—Chocolate Can Boost Your IQ!"; "Are Night Owls More Creative?"; and, "What Is Wi-Fi And How Does It Work?" are essays that are intended to be rest stops or R&R from the rigor of highly focused reading.

My hope is that you have heard and will heed that "silent voice" within Concepts of Intelligence—the voice that addresses you as an individual, and not as a subject in an experimental or a control group. Whether you are male or female; young or old; extrovert or introvert; you are very special and capable. You give form and purpose to your thinking, and your hopes and goals define the future. Discovery and creativity march forward with you at your own measured pace. You are, indeed, the center of the universe. Discover, unearth, investigate, study, understand and enlighten us.

REFERENCES:

Birth Order and Intelligence:

[1]   London: Macmillan, 1874.

[2]   Galton did not count female children when he reported the results; so, theoretically, a boy could be considered the "first born" even if he was the last born, providing that his older siblings were all females.

[3]   A longitudinal study is a correlational research study that involves repeated observations of the same items over long periods of time, often many decades.

[4]   Cross-sectional studies (also known as Cross-sectional analysis) form a class of research methods that involve observation of some subset of a population of items all at the same time in which groups can be compared at different ages with respect of independent variables, such as IQ and memory. The fundamental difference between cross-sectional and longitudinal studies is that cross-sectional studies take place at a single point in time and that a longitudinal study involves a series of measurements taken over a period of time. Both are a type of observational study.

[5]   Thomas Hally. "Are we smarter than Our Ancestors?—the Flynn Effect," *Mensa International Journal*, September 2008, issue number 518, pp. 1-2. Ed. Kate Nacard.

[6] Thomas Hally. "Are we smarter than Our Ancestors? — the Flynn Effect," *Mensa International Journal, September* 2008, issue number 518, pp. 1-2. Ed. Kate Nacard.

[7] The resource dilution model posits that parental resources are finite and that as the number of children in the family increases, the resources accrued by any one child necessarily decline.

[8] Zajonc, R.B. & Markus, G. (1975). "Birth order and intellectual development." *Psychological Review*, 82, 74-88.

[9] As more children enter the family, the general intellectual environment becomes less mature.

[10] Even within science, IQ is only weakly related to achievement among people who are intelligent enough to become scientists. Research has shown, for example, that a scientist who has an IQ of 130 may be just as likely to win a Nobel Prize as a scientist whose IQ is 180. (Hudson, L., 1966). *Contrary Imaginations: A Psychological Study of the English Schoolboy.* London: Methuen.

Creative Genius Or Psychotic?:

[11] www.sma.org.sg/sma_news/3403/commentary.pdf.

[12] Ibid.

Are We Smarter than Our Ancestors? — the Flynn Effect:

[13] Flynn, James R., *What is Intelligence? Beyond the Flynn Effect*. New York: Cambridge University Press, 200.

Howard Gardner's Theory of Multiple Intelligences:

[14]   www.mitest.com/o7inte~htm.

[15]   http://www.moreintelligentlife.com/node/654

Moctezuma's Revenge—Chocolate Can Boost Your IQ! :

[16]   http://www.nottingham.ac.uk/public-affairs/
       press-releases/index.phtml?menu=pr.

[17]   Selfgrowth.com, Self Improvement on line, Inc.

Men With Smarts are Men Who Win Hearts:

[18]   Oxford English Dictionary. Oxford University Press
       2009.

[19]   http://www.unm.edu/~psych/faculty/lg_gmiller.html.

[20]   http://www.northumbria.ac.uk/browse/ne/
       uninews/1127841.

Phrenology: Protoscience/Pseudoscience:

[21]   This rudimentary concept eventually gave rise to the
       theory of "brain localization" which was proven by the
       time computers came into the picture.

Are Beautiful People More Intelligent?:

[22]   Satoshi Kanazawa and Jody L. Kovar, "Why beautiful
       people are more intelligent." Available online at www.
       sciencedirect.com.

23 The *halo effect* refers to a cognitive bias whereby the perception of a particular trait is influenced by the perception of the former traits in a sequence of interpretations.

24 I would suggest striking up a conversation with one of the beautiful "gods" or "goddesses" who frequent Malibu Beach, near Los Angeles, California to test the accuracy of these assumptions.

25 Critics of the KK theorem have believe that many extremely attractive women are unintelligent, noting that, in the ancestral environment, light blonde hair and large firm breasts, for example, were indicators of youth and thus gave the impression of naïveté and inexperience, which was interpreted as lack of intelligence. A recent term for young women who actually fit this stereotype is "bimbo" or "bimbette."

26 A few works authored by Dr. Satoshi Kanazawa:

Kanazawa, Satoshi and Diane J. Reyniers. 2009."The Role of Height in the Sex Difference in Intelligence." *American Journal of Psychology;*
Kanazawa, Satoshi and Kaja Perina. 2009. "Why Night Owls Are More Intelligent." *Personality and Individual Differences;*
Kanazawa, Satoshi. 2007. "Beautiful Parents Have More Daughters: A Further Implication of the Generalized Trivers-Willard Hypothesis (gTWH)." *Journal of Theoretical Biology;*
Kanazawa, Satoshi. 2010. "Why Liberals and Atheists Are More Intelligent." *Social Psychology Quarterly.* 73 (1).

[27] The *naturalistic fallacy* is often claimed to be a formal fallacy. It was described and named by British philosopher G.E. Moore in his 1903 book *Principia Ethica*. Moore stated that a naturalistic fallacy was committed whenever a philosopher attempts to prove a claim about ethics by appealing to a *definition* of the term "good" in terms of one or more *natural* properties such as "pleasant," "more evolved," "desired," etc. The naturalistic fallacy is related to, and often confused with, the "is-ought problem," and comes from Hume's *Treatise*. As a result, the term is sometimes used loosely to describe arguments that claim to draw ethical conclusions from natural facts.

[28] UCD School of Economics & Geary Institute, University College Dublin, Belfeld, Dublin 4, Republic of Ireland (Eire).

[29] Dr. Kevin Denny, UCD Geary Institute Discussion Paper Series, "Beauty and Intelligence may or may not be related." P2.

The Mozart Effect:

[30] The term "Mozart Effect" was coined by the media in response to a study by Dr. Frances Rauscher and Dr. Gordon Shaw and their colleagues of the University of California at Irvine in 1993.

[31] Gordon L. Shaw, Academic Press, 84 Theobold's Road (London, WCIX 8RR, UK 2004, 2000).

[32] The Case for Music in the Schools," Phi Delta Kappan, February, 1994.

[33] Source: *Houston Chronicle*, January 11, 1998.

Personality and Creativity: Extroversion vs. Introversion:

[34]   Jung, C.G. *Psychological Types* (1921); H.Eysenck, ed., *A Model for Personality* (1981).

[35]   findarticles.com/p/articles/mi_m0846/is_5_23/ ai_111518927 Fleeson, W. "Towards a Structure-and Process-Integrated View of Personality: Traits as Density Distributions of States." *Journal of Personality and Social Psychology*, 80, (2001): 1011-1027.

[36]   www.psychologytoday.com/articles/pto-1095.html From *Creativity: The Work and Lives of 91 Eminent People*, by Mihaly Csikszentmihalyi, published by HarperCollins, 1996.

[37]   Sir Isaac Newton.

[38]   Those interested in taking the test can find it in the "articles" link, the I-E Scale at www.mysteriumsociety.org.

[39]   www.keirsey.com/sorter/register.aspx.

[40]   www.humanmetrics.com/cgi-win/JTypes2.asp.

Neural Networks: An Overview:

[41]   Neuroimaging: Imaging 1. Any imaging technique—eg, PET scans, functional MRI, used to evaluate functional aspects of neural activity 2. Images obtained from the head which detect any abnormal mass, but which do not identify a specific type of tumor.
       McGraw-Hill Concise Dictionary of Modern Medicine © 2002 by The McGraw-Hill Companies, Inc.

[42]   Den·drite n. Any of the various branched protoplasmic extensions of a nerve cell that conducts impulses from adjacent cells inward toward the cell body. Also

called *dendritic process*, *dendron*, *neurodendrite*, *neurodendron*. The American Heritage® Medical Dictionary Copyright © 2007, 2004 by Houghton Mifflin Company. Published by Houghton Mifflin Company. All rights reserved.

[43] Axon: n (Life Sciences & Allied Applications / Biology) the long threadlike extension of a nerve cell that conducts nerve impulses from the cell body.

[via New Latin from Greek: axis, axle, vertebra].

axonal adj.

Collins English Dictionary Complete and Unabridged. HarperCollins Publishers 1991, 1994, 1998, 2000, 2003.

[44] Syn·apse n. The junction across which a nerve impulse passes from an axon terminal to a neuron, muscle cell, or gland cell. intr.v. syn·apsed, syn·aps·ing, syn·aps·es.

1. To form a synapse.

2. To undergo synapsis. [Greek sunapsis, *point of contact*, from sunaptein, *to join together*: sun-, *syn-* + haptein, *to fasten*].

The American Heritage® Dictionary of the English Language, Fourth Edition copyright ©2000 by Houghton Mifflin Company. Updated in 2009. Published by Houghton Mifflin Company. All rights reserved.

[45] Turing-B:

www.alanturing.net/turing.../Turing's%20neural%20 networks.html.

[46] Perceptron: http://tinyurl.com/7hzgke5.

[47] Fredrich August von Hayek was an Austrian-born economist and philosopher known for his defense of classical liberalism and free-market capitalism. Hayek

also wrote on the topics of neuroscience and the history of ideas.

[48] Cognitron: http://tinyurl.com/6vd8d8z.

[49] A Hopfield Network is a form of recurrent artificial neural network invented by John Hopfield, an American scientist known for his invention of an *associative neural network* in 1982.

[50] Parallel Distribution: The Parallel Distributed Processing Model is a relatively new model regarding the processes of memory. The model postulates that information is not inputted into the memory system in a step by step manner like most models or theories hypothesize but instead, facts or images are distributed to all parts in the memory system at once. Older models hypothesized that information would consolidate first into sensory memory, then move to short-term memory, and then finally go to long-term memory.

[51] George Siemens, "Connectivism: A Learning Theory for the Digital Age," *International Journal of Industrial Technology and Distance Learning,* vol. 2, no. 1, January 2005, 3.

[52] D.E. Rumelhart, G.E. Hinton, and R.J. Williams, *"Learning Internal Representation by Error Propagation"* (Technical report: University of California San Diego La Jolla Institute for Cognitive Science. March-September, 1985).

[53] http://www.themeasurementgroup.com/.../logistic_regression.html.

[54] Multilayer Perceptron: A network composed of more than one layer of neurons, with some or all of the outputs of each layer connected to one or more of the inputs of another layer. The first layer is called the input layer, the last one is the output layer, and

in between there may be one or more hidden layers. Free online Computing Dictionary (foldoc.org).

55 Bayesian Inference: http://www.fact-index.com/b/ba/bayesian_inference.html.

56 Fourier Transform: the Fourier Theorem states that any waveform can be duplicated by the superposition of a series of sine and cosine waves.

57 Expert System: http://www.iiia.csic.es/udt/en/artificialintelligence/list?page=1.

58 Estimation: Estimation Theory (statistics). A branch of probability and statistics concerned with deriving information about properties of random variables, stochastic processes, and systems based on observed samples.
McGraw-Hill Dictionary of Scientific & Technical Terms, 6E, Copyright © 2003 by The McGraw-Hill Companies, Inc.

59 Optimization: Collins English Dictionary—Complete and Unabridged© HarperCollins Publishers 1991, 1994, 1998, 2000, 2003. optimize, optimise.
1. *(tr)* to take the full advantage of.
2. (Business / Commerce) *(tr)* to plan or carry out (an economic activity) with maximum efficiency.
3. *(intr)* to be optimistic.
4. (Electronics & Computer Science / Computer Science) *(tr)* to write or modify (a computer program) to achieve maximum efficiency in storage capacity, time, cost, etc.
5. *(tr)* to find the best compromise among several often conflicting requirements, as in engineering design.
optimization, optimisation n.

60 Control Theory: <a href="http://www.thefreedictionary.com/Control+theory">Control theory</a>

61 Mass, Wolfgang and Bishop, Christopher M., "Pulsed Neural Networks": (Massachusetts Institute of Technology, 1999), XXV.

62 José Félix Rodriguez Jiménez, Senior Software Engineer, ContPAQ I, Guadalajara, Jalisco, Mexico.

Does Our Creativity Decline as We Grow Older?:

63 Far from being a bad thing, academic knowledge is the key that opens the world to creativity and divergent thinking. The problem is that rote learning and creativity oftentimes do not coalesce. Our abilities to reinvent and excel can be inhibited when we are young, and university instructors may discard or label many of our creative ideas as "bohemian" or "non-conformist."

64 An operating definition of *cognitive trap* from www.creatingminds.org: Opinions and feelings as a substitute for good thinking; defining your reality by what you know, what you believe, and how you act.

65 http://www.expotv.com/videos/reviews/4/53/The-Creative-Age-Awakening-Human-Potent/65978.

66 History informs us that Sophocles wrote *Oedipus at Colonus* when he was 89, and United States Supreme Court Justice, Oliver Wendell Holmes, began his studies in Greek at the age of 92.

67 *Crystallized intelligence* can be considered as the ever-increasing sum of learning during a lifetime of varied and continuous experiences.

68 Collins, Glenn "Exploring the Past: Creativity in Old Age," *The New York Times*. March 2, 1981.

[69] One of the most consistent markers of longevity across the wworld, in all economic conditions, is higher education. If you stay in school and get a degree, it seems to increase your chances of living longer more than almost anything else, apart from taking physical care of yourself with regular exercise, eating healthy, and not smoking. As technology and medicine evolve over time, the life expectancies in most countries are increasing.

[70] Here are a few additional ways of increasing the odds that you will make it to that ripe old age of 85 and beyond: www.wikihow.com/Live-a-Long-Life.

IQ, Intelligence, Ethnicity and Gender:

[71] Thomas Hally. "Are We Smarter Than Our Ancestors? —The Flynn Effect," Mensa International Journal. September 2008, issue 518, pp. 1-2. Ed. Kate Nacard.

[72] *IQ and the Wealth of Nations* by Dr. Richard Lynn, Professor Emeritus of Psychology at the University of Ulster, Northern Ireland and Dr. Tatu Vanhanen, Professor Emeritus of Political Science at the University of Tampere, Tampere, Finland.

[73] http://web.archive.org/web/20080130023006/

[74] http://www.president.harvard.edu/speeches/2005/nber.html.

[75] In 1956, Shockley was a Nobel Prize winner in physics, but he was also a radical eugenics advocate and considered an extremist for his belief in Black intellectual inferiority.

[76] The Connection Machine utilizes 65000 computers linked in parallel to form the fastest computer on Earth. This computer can perform 3.1 billion calculations per

second. This is faster than the theoretical top speed of the Cray Supercomputer.

[77] As it turns out, 104 is the average IQ of Taiwan, the third highest national average on the list of the nations that were in the study.

The Ups and Downs of Emotional Intelligence:

[78] Alan Ginsberg is the author of *Howl*, a bestselling book of free flow style poetry and "free association," a method Sigmund Freud used in psychoanalysis.

Critical Thinking, Creative Thinking and Genius:

[79] The conception derives from the opening of the Gospel of John, commonly translated into English as: "In the beginning was the Word, and the Word was with God, and the Word was God."

[80] The presentations or expositions of facts, beliefs or suppositions (presumptions) are also arguments inasmuch as they can be challenged, analyzed, and synthesized and their truth or falsehood can be extrapolated, creating new concepts and [eventual] arguments, moving in the same manner as *The Hegelian Dialectic*.

[81] Huitt, W. (1998). "Critical Thinking: An Overview." *Educational Psychology Interactive,* p. 1. Valdosa, GA. Valdosa State University.

[82] Ibid. p. 2.

[83] The Hegelian dialectic is an interpretive method, originally used to relate specific entities or events to the

absolute idea, in which an assertable proposition *(thesis)* is necessarily opposed by its apparent contradiction *(antithesis),* and both reconciled on a higher level of truth by a third proposition *(synthesis)*. Also called Hegelian triad. From, *The Free Dictionary,* Farlex.

84 The Stanford Encyclopedia of Philosophy, "*The Language of Thought Hypothesis*":

The *Language of Thought Hypothesis* (LOTH) postulates that thought and thinking take place in a mental language. This language consists of a system of representations that is physically realized in the brain of thinkers and has a combinatorial syntax (and semantics) such that operations on representations are causally sensitive only to the syntactic properties of representations. According to LOTH, thought is, roughly, the tokening of a representation that has a syntactic (constituent) structure with an appropriate semantics. Thinking thus consists in syntactic operations defined over such representations. Most of the arguments for LOTH derive their strength from their ability to explain certain empirical phenomena like productivity and systematicity of thought and thinking.

85 Jean Marrapodi, "Critical Thinking and Creativity an Overview and Comparison of the Theories." Independent Researcher.

86 Convergent thinking is generally linear thinking in a step-by-step manner. Divergent thinking is non-linear thinking (lateral thinking) or that which is now commonly known as "out-of-the-box" thinking.

87 Since a valid goal for creativity can be art for art's sake (*L'art pour L'art*), in this case, the end does justify the means.

[88] GIGO = Originally an acronym in computer programming argot meaning Garbage In/Garbage Out. Describes the logically expected results of a computer program when faulty or poor input outputs faulty or poor output or results.

Personality and Creativity:

[89] Convergent thinking or intelligence is the kind of intelligence measured by conventional IQ tests. Convergent intelligence helps the artist; poet, sculptor, and writer differentiate good ideas from poor ones.

[90] Divergent thinking is thinking "outside [of] the box." Divergent thinking is a deviation from the norm (convergent thinking). It is the kind of thinking that creative people use to solve problems and produce their works of art.

The Rise and Fall of the World's IQ:

[91] Kaiser Wilhelm Institut fuer Anthoropologie, menschliche Erblehre und Eugenik.

[92] Herrnstein, Richard J. and Charles Murray, *The Bell Curve: Intelligence and Class Structure in American Life*. (1994). New York: Random House.

[93] Inherited. The genotype of an organism is the inherited instructions it carries within its genetic code.

[94] A phenotype is an organism's observable characteristics or traits such as its morphology development, biochemical or physiological properties, behavior and products of behavior.

[95] Author of "The Flynn Effect and 'g.'"

[96] Robert Lindsey, September 14, 2009. 5:16 A.M. "The Flynn Effect and 'g'." Repost from the old site.

97 Griswold, Alan "Autistic Songs" © 2011.

98 Ibid.

99 Lynn, R. and Harvey, J. *Intelligence* 36 (2008) p.15.

The Optimist's Advantage:

100 Richard Wiseman, PhD., is a psychologist from the University of Hertfordshire in England, and the author of *The Luck Factor*. The quotation cited is from that online *Psychology Today* article: www.psychologytoday.com/print/42128.

101 *Weltanschauung* is a German noun adopted in its original form into the English language, and it means "world view" in the sense of either an adopted "philosophy of life" by a particular person, or the more general outlook shared by a nation or people in a given period. E.g., What was the Weltanschauung of Nazi Germany?

102 m-w.com.

103 Seize the Day is commonly expressed using the original Latin expression: *Carpe Diem.*

104 The World English Dictionary (online) defines a Pollyanna as one who finds a cause for gladness in the most difficult situations. (1921): This is an allusion to Pollyanna Whittier, child heroine of US novelist Eleanor Hodgeman Porter's *Pollyanna* (1913) and *Pollyanna Grows Up* (1915), and noted for keeping her chin up and being a ("somewhat impossible") optimist with unrealistic expectations during disasters.

105 Joseph Forgas is a Professor of Psychology at the University of New South Wales. He is also a Doctor of Science. Both his doctorates were earned at Oxford University, England.

106 Joseph Forgas, PhD., "Feeling Grumpy is Good for You," story from BBC NEWS: http://news.bbc.co.uk/go/pr/fr/hi/health/8339647.stm, published: 2009/11/05 17:15:23 GMT © 2011.

107 Psychcentral.com/blog/ archives/2011/03/17pessimism-vs-optimism.

108 An alarmist; scaremonger, or a "Henny Penny." If you are not familiar with the story of Chicken Little, I suggest you "Google it!"

The *G*-Factor:

109 The *g*-factor, where "*g*" stands for "general intelligence," is measured by statistical methods used in psychometrics and is a model of mental ability underlying results of various tests of cognitive ability. First developed in 1904 by Spearman to account for imperfect correlations in IQ tests, this model is considered the first theory of intelligence.

110 Spearman's Two-Factor Theory of intelligence introduced "factor analysis" into the statistics of psychology. Charles Spearman is sometimes credited with the invention of factor analysis.

111 Other highly g-loaded tests are the Wechsler Adult Intelligence Scale (WAIS) and the Wechsler Intelligence Scale for Children (WISC).

112 MRI: *Magnetic Resonance Imaging.* An MRI (magnetic resonance imaging) scan is a imaging test that uses powerful magnets and radio waves to create pictures of the body. It does not use radiation (x-rays). *Medicine Plus Medical Encyclopedia.*

[113] Tucker-Drob, E. M. (2009)." Differentiation of cognitive abilities across the life span", *Developmental Psychology*, 45, 1097-1118.

[114] Jensen, A.R., (1998) *The G Factor.*

[115] Bouchard, T.J.Jr., "Genetic Influence on Human Intelligence (Spearman's g): How Much?" 2009 Sep-Oct; 36(5):527-44. Psychology Department, University of Minnesota, Minneapolis, MN 55455-0344, USA. bouch001@umn.edu.

[116] Magnetic Resonance Imaging.

[117] I wonder if mathematician John Forbes Nash has a typically genius-level IQ, like most Nobel Prize winners, or if he has *even taken* an IQ test . . .? Bear in mind that Nash has a severe problem with schizophrenia, as did poet Jack Kerouac (What was *his* IQ . . .?). There is plenty of evidence that schizophrenic thought is similar in many ways to "genius-pattern" thinking; much the same as some creative individuals with bipolar disorder.

[118] Gottfredson, Linda S. "The General Intelligence Factor." Scientific American (online).

[119] Thomas Hally. "Howard Gardner's Theory of Multiple Intelligences," *Mensa International Journal*, August, 2008. Issue 517. Ed. Kate Nacard.

Intelligent Intuition:

[120] Root-Bernstein, Michele and Robert. Intuition and the Logic of Sensual Thinking," *Psychology Today.* (http://psychologytoday.com) Feb 28 2011 — 12:33 p.m.

[121] "The Powers and Perils of Intuition," *Psychology Today.* http://www.psychologytoday.com/node/23438.

Genetics, Intelligence and Environment:

122 He is known as "The Father of Eugenics."

123 dNate.com (The nexus of politics, culture and genetics): Myth: Human behavioral traits are 50% genetic and 50% environmental.

124 Building upon our genetic inheritance and linking it to our present environment.

125 Environment (nurture) proponents in the nature versus nurture debate.

126 He is known as "The Father of Behavioral Science."

127 David Brooks, *The New York Times.*

128 Criminal behavior must not be condoned. Excusing one's actions because of genetic makeup should not be taken into consideration in a court of law. Self-discipline and moral responsibility is exercised in order to redirect one's natural (negative) inclinations. We are ultimately responsible for our actions.

129 (University of Manchester). Published in *Molecular Psychology.*

130 ScienceDaily. http://www.sciencedaily.com/ releases/2011/08/1/0811215420.htm.

131 Ibíd.

132 A new Harvard study (2012) has found that most of the genes thought to be linked to Intelligence are probably not, in fact, related to it.

133 Obsid.

134 With our mug (face) on one side of the fence, and our wump ("rump," backside) on the other.

Multiple Intelligences:

[135] The challenge posed for the future is the development of a theory that makes g compatible with the apparent level of simplicity in intellectual functioning that Howard Gardner describes.

[136] Sternberg came to the conclusion that although performance components contribute to individual differences in intelligence, overall the contribution is weak, since correlations rarely exceed 0.3.